# THE
# MAINE
# COAST

PORTRAITS OF AMERICA

# THE
# MAINE
# COAST

GEORGE PUTZ

CHARTWELL
BOOKS, INC.

A QUINTET BOOK

Published by Chartwell Books Inc.,
A Division of Book Sales Inc.,
114 Northfield Avenue,
Edison, New Jersey 08837

ISBN 0-89009-882-4

Reprinted 1994, 1996

This book was designed and produced by
Quintet Publishing Limited
6 Blundell Street, London N7
in association with Footnote
Productions Limited

Art Director Peter Bridgewater
Editor Sheila Rosenzweig
Photographer Peter Ralston

Typeset in Great Britain by
Leaper & Gard Limited, Bristol
Colour origination in Hong Kong by
Hong Kong Graphic Arts Company Limited,
Hong Kong
Printed in China by Leefung-Asco
Printers Limited

For George Hoyt Putz and Alyce
Lovas Putz, my parents, who in their retirement at
Half Moon Bay are neighbors on
the World Ocean. As Dad, a native Midwesterner,
once said "It doesn't matter what
coast—just that it is a coast." Visiting the coast of
Maine for the first time, he also said,
"Yup, this is *it*."

# CONTENTS

# THE MAINE COAST

BELFA

Lincc

Damariscotta
Lake

CAMDEN

ROCKPORT

ROCKLAND

WALDOBORO

THOMASTON

Newcastle

Broad Cove

Cushing

Saint George

WISCASSET

FRIENDSHIP

Spruce He

LEWISTON

Edgecomb

Bristol

Woolwich

Tenants Harbor

Walpole Roundpond

Sebago
Lake

BRUNSWICK

BATH

Pemaquid

Boothbay

New Harbor

Desert of Maine

Phippsburg

Southport
Island

YARMOUTH

Georgetown

Parker Head

Muscongus Bay

Monhegan Island

Orrs Island

M

Chebeague
Island

Harpswell

Popham Beach

FALMOUTH

Bailey Island

Eagle
Island

Small Point Beach

WESTBROOK

Casco Bay

PORTLAND

Portland Head Light

Two Lights

CAPE ELIZABETH

SACO

PROUTS NECK

SPRINGVALE

BIDDEFORD

OLD ORCHARD BEACH

Saco Bay

SANFORD

KENNEBUNK

KENNEBUNKPORT

BERWICK

SOMERSWORTH

CAPE NEDDICK

ELIOT

YORK

KITTERY

PORTSMOUTH

**CALAIS**

Perry

Pembroke

**EASTPORT**

Dennisville

*Cobscook Bay*

Moosehorn National
Wildlife Refuge

**MACHIAS**

Machiasport

Bucks Harbor

Cutler

**BANGOR**

Cherryfield

Harrington

Addison

Rocque Bluffs

*Rocque Island*

*Machias
Bay*

Fort Knox

**BUCKSPORT**

**ELLSWORTH**

**MILBRIDGE**

Jonesport

*Chandler Bay*

Surry

*Dyer
Island*

Point

Fort Pownall

Lamoine

Sorrento

*Pleasant
Bay*

*Dyers Bay*

Trenton

Hancock Point

*Sears
Island*

**WINTER
HARBOR**

Prospect Harbor

**PETIT MANAN POINT**

Castine

**BLUE HILL**

**BAR HARBOR**

Mt. Desert

Acadia

Birch Harbor

Corea

Eggemoggin

National

**CADILLAC
MTN.**

Park

Seal Harbor

**SPRUCE POINT**

*Schoodic Island*

Sedgwick

*Little Dear
Island*

Brooklin

Tremont

**NORTHEAST
HARBOR**

*Frenchman Bay*

*Butter
Island*

*Eagle
Island*

Bass Harbor

*Jericho Bay*

*Swans Island*

*Obscot Bay*

*North Haven
Island*

*Isle
Au Haut
Bay*

Frenchboro

*Long Island*

s Head

**VINALHAVEN**

Acadia
National
Park

*Green
Island*

*Seal Island*

s Island

*Wooden Ball Island*

d Island

Criehaven

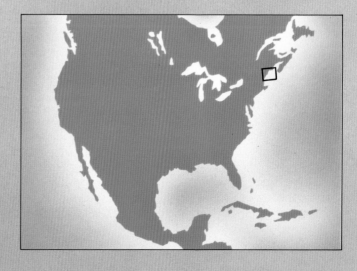

# INTRODUCTION

The Piscataqua. Across this river lies Strawberry Bank and Portsmouth, New Hampshire. Below us is Kittery Harbor—small, with a few yachts, the mighty Atlantic to the left, wild Gerrish Island around the corner and the Isles of Shoals beyond. Off to the right and along the river shore is the Kittery Navy Yard, where ancient trades and our highest technologies converge in the construction of nuclear submarines. Behind us sits one of America's oldest communities, still infused with life and pride, skates and bicycles, elegance, people assured of their sense of place. It is the beginning of the Maine coast. Turning around, we will follow this extra-ordinary shore, and such a journey it is! Encompassing only a few hundred linear miles between Kittery to the west and Eastport at the easterly end of the coast, the "mean high-water line" of Maine's mainland shore is fully 2,500 miles long! Indented with a myriad of bays, coves, and river channels, it is quite common along the coast to be able to stand on a point of land, looking over to another point of land—say, a 30-minute trip away by row-boat—and yet be faced with the prospect of an hour and a half's drive by automobile to the same nearby point. Time and again we will see that the Maine coast is first and foremost a maritime place, not simply because it is *by* that sea but also because, in many ways, it is very thoroughly *of* the sea.

At the westerly end of the shore, at Kittery, we stand at a threshold of American history. The river mouth has many old forts of a half-dozen eras, from the French and Indian War period of the mid-eighteenth century to World War II observation bunkers, with all other conflict period installations from the 200-year interim. Indeed, the whole area is a popular retirement region for military officers, who understandably like to pursue the history of their profession once their tours of active duty have ended. And everywhere, too, are signs of the ancient New World ways of life that these forts protected. Whole neighborhoods in the area predate the Revolutionary War. Indeed, you can be sure that many of the very old bottles, which commonly line household windowsills of the older homes, were more likely found by the occupants while gardening in their backyards than purchased in the antique barns and shops that abound in the area.

Relic places of early American trade, manufacturing, and certainly farming are everywhere right and left along the roadways of the westerly coast. By the way, before we get too far along on our journey, it should be pointed out that the instinct to think of the Maine shore to be "up north" of everywhere else along the Eastern Seaboard is not one shared by Mainers, for distinctly nautical reasons. Looking at a map or nautical chart, the coast is seen to run more or less northeast/southwest, depending on perspective. But it was for sailors, who have to carry on their affairs by time, tide, and the wind, the general prevailing southwest sailing breeze, the navigational requirements of "clearing" points of land, and the compass deviation between *true* and *magnetic* north, that the literal phrases "to sail *downeast*" and/or "up t' th' westward" were created.

The nature of early American trade and farming easily explain the importance of what is now southern and western Maine in the early days, and why the area around and up-river of Kittery was so crucial in Colonial times. We in the modern era may find it difficult to grasp how truly terrible early road travel was. Most roads were no more than Indian trails; for wheeled traffic plain bad in summer; impassable in winter. So water transport was the preferred and often only viable means to move people and goods from place to place. Farms, then tended to be first established on or near protected coves and rivers, and usually at sites previously occupied by Indians, where exposures to sun, desirable (against insects!) summer breezes, cleared land (the Indians were farmers, too), and the ability to observe and be forewarned against attack, all contributed to making certain places especially desirable. But, first, the place had to be near navigable water.

*Early History*

Maine was, until 1820, part and parcel of the Massachusetts Bay Colony, with headquarters

The small **red-breasted merganser** is one of a high number of water fowl that can be spotted in Maine. It lives on fish which give its flesh so rank a taste that sportsmen call it 'trash duck'.

in Boston, largely due to that town's fine harbor. But the rivers that empty into Boston Harbor are relatively short, and their watersheds were soon settled and accounted for. Early records describe much of the region in back of Boston to be undesirable marsh and swamp. Central and western Massachusetts were settled along the Connecticut River, an area whose north/south trade was of greater benefit to the Long Island Sound area and New York City than to mother Boston. The Piscataqua River drainage, on the other hand, was relatively vast, and the farmers who exploited its watershed and transport facility soon joined up inland with those who had followed up the Concord and Merrimack River systems to make up New England's primary breadbasket. Had the English not kept Boston as its premier administrative center (and, possibly, had the New Hampshire Crown Governors not been so greedy), Mainers might very well have found themselves much closer to the civil hub of the New England colonies. Certainly many citizens of early Portsmouth and Falmouth (Portland) would have wanted it that way, since the bulk of them seem to have displaced themselves down east not simply for its hydraulic resources but also to get out from under the thumb of Boston's pugnacious Puritanism—a sense not altogether extinct to this very day!

As it was, Maine's early westernmost settlers got their goods to market at places like Portsmouth where, often as not, they found themselves gouged by a mixture of clever traders and elaborate licensing schemes that required transshipment to Boston, bonding, and so on, the ire over which eventually resulted in the American Revolution and familiar history. We shall return to this when we tour the Saco River Basin.

## Conflicts with The Indians

This was *part* of the problem. Besides which, and more serious for the principals involved, there were difficulties with the Indians. The coast of Maine, as for all of New England, has been host to human habitation for over 7,000 years. Most everyone who lives on the coast, or explores it seriously, knows of at least one Indian site nearby. There are many hundreds of them, and, much to the chagrin of the region's professional archaeologists, amateur digging in these sites for artifacts, "arrowheads" generally, constitutes a common coastal hobby. Over the centuries and millennia, many different cultures and lifestyles were established, flourished, and then disappeared to become a "period" in the archaeological record—some just fleeting glimpses, others leaving extensive and spectacular "middensites," such as the massive oyster shell mounds of the Damariscotta River Basin. In any case, Indians were everywhere throughout the region for a very long time.

For many years, it was believed that Maine's Indian groups simply visited the coastal shores during summer and then regrouped in the upland areas for winter. Recent archaeological work has shown this belief to be incorrect for many periods, and indeed it may be a rationalization created by the early settlers and historians to justify the occupation of Indian lands. All scientific indications are that New England's indigenous peoples fished, farmed, and hunted in their own version of what modern occupants call the "salt-water farm."

## The Impact of European Settlers

This lifestyle was quickly decimated by the arrival of European settlers, first by disease, then trade, and finally by force of arms. First, the urbanizing and far Eastern trade developments of the later European Middle Ages provided an ideal environment for the creation of pandemic disease organisms to which the later New World settlers had become largely immune, but nevertheless carried. The Indians were not immune. Historical sources say that over 75 percent of their populations were killed by these diseases in the closing decades of the seventeenth century—a radical figure that brought radical changes!

Then, when the new white trading networks had been established, and the Indians had entered them as traders in the pelts for which European markets were voracious, the coastal animal stocks on which this trade depended were quickly exhausted. This by necessity transformed the resident coastal Indians from hunting-fishing-farming people into transient traders and marauders, acting as liaisons between the white communities on the coast and the Indian groups with viable peltries in the vast interior. To protect this trading arrangement, the "middle Indians," those Indian groups in the interior at the head of navigable rivers, soon formed themselves into large intertribal confederations designed to keep the supply-Indians, who lived inland, from trading directly with the demand-whites in the maritime trading and market centers. Indian militarization, in other words, was created to protect a middle-man position between whites, and other Indians. This is why Indians native to upstate New York became participants in Maine coast massacres.

Boon Island, offshore of Maine's westerly coastline **left**, was the site of one of early America's great scandals, immortalized in Kenneth Roberts novel *Boon Island.* here a midwinter shipwreck brought together a diverse ship's company, some of whom ate the others, calling the homogenous fare "beef." A most towering light was built soon afterward.

## The French Colonialists

The French, of course, were directly involved. Unlike the English settlers, who clung tenaciously to their ships, harbors, and farms, the French colonialists were much more terrestrially mobile, and early on sent missionary and trade tentacles into the continental interior. In the process, they forged very good relations with the interior Indian groups. These good relationships were soon brought into play by the French in their continuing dispute with the English over colonial territory. And the coast of Maine was caught right in the middle.

Though the Maine coastal Indian groups were themselves quickly brought to subservience as groups, many individual Indians adopted privateering lifestyles, and the intricate network of Indian trails that reached into the interior over the "height of land" in the White Mountains was continually exploited by them, in league with the French, to harass and generally render unviable any easy or profitable settlement of most of the coast of Maine. Indeed, east of Casco Bay (and its towns of Falmouth, Yarmouth, and Brunswick), life was generally hazardous, and development of the sort experienced by the townships westward of it was delayed for nearly a century. There was plenty of settlement, to be sure, but it was done slowly and with a great deal of anxiety. And the upshot of it was that Maine was subsequently always considered to be a territory to be exploited for its resources rather than a hub of civility. Mainers were people of resources and skills rather than principals in empirical development.

## Todays Villages

This brings us back to the villages along the westward shores of Maine. They, like their people, are a product of their special history.

Villages were always established where and how they are by virtue of the accessibility to surrounding farms and timber resources, on the one hand, and good deep-water, protected anchorage and wharfage bank for shipping, on the other hand. As we walk through the centers of these towns, we generally find them up on a knoll above the docks some distance, and as we drive through them we must imagine them with far fewer trees than are seen now—in most cases, with no trees at all. Those trees we see now were planted late in history—at the turn of this century.

The houses we see were built by merchants, tradesmen, traders and shippers, on lots assigned to them by formal commissions established for that purpose. Nearby there is a square or common, originally designed for common grazing of draft animals owned by people visiting for trade purposes. A square was also designed as a place of public forum, including punishment for misdemeanor. Each house would have a barn and a carriage house for driving stock. In the early days, each home would be surrounded by a thoroughly sound picket fence that guarded against pigs, which by common practice were always sent out free to forage, catch-as-catch-can, all over the township.

When you look at a Maine coastal village, you *see* the past. Protection, farming, trade, shipping, society, and even pigs, even though the fences may be no more than a soil-stain around the well-mown lawns that once were intensively cultivated gardens. Today's elegant realty villages were once much more prosaic, active, and smelly. They were, once, America.

Many coastal townships have local historical societies and museums devoted to their unique pasts. The many small but well-subscribed atheneums and libraries that dot the coast usually specialize in local lore, for the coast of Maine has attracted writers and inspired literary efforts, historical and otherwise, almost from the beginnings of white settlement. Visiting and reading it all has become a lifetime pursuit for many, seasonal visitors and coastal residents alike. We will touch on a few historical highlights, here and there, where germane on our coastal journey, but these few fundamentals are common to all the coast and infuse the present geography of the region, and so receive our attentions here.

**Opposite** The long, wide expanse of smooth sand of the beach at York makes it among Maine's, and the world's, finest. Nubble Light is near by.

**Northern Cardinal** This bright red-crested bird is America's most spectacular finch. It can be seen in gardens and woodland edges.

# THE WESTERLY SHORE OF CAPE ELIZABETH

York County is Maine's oldest for the very good reason that from 1652, when it was established by the Massachusetts Bay Colony's General Court, until 1760, when "Yorkshire" was subdivided into Cumberland and Lincoln and York Counties, it occupied the entire area we call Maine today. In the same 1652 session that instituted Yorkshire County, the townships of Kittery, first settled in 1623, and York, settled the next year, became the first and second officially incorporated townships in the province. This must have been an irksome embarrassment to the York people, who up until that year had been called Gorgeana (after Sir Ferdinando Gorges, whose heirs owned virtually all of Maine until 1677) and had in 1641 been chartered as "the first English city in America" by the homeland Parliament. Win some, lose some . . . .

All of Maine's coast is so rife with "firsts" in American history that to attempt more than the more cursory mention of a few, now and then, is beyond the scope of this coastal portrait. And what is true of the coast generally is even more true of this westerly coastal area. Here are a few firsts: Maine's first Quaker meeting was held at Newichawannock, now South Berwick, in 1662; the first Quaker meetinghouse was built in Eliot in 1776; Maine's first schoolhouse was built at Berwick in 1719; Madam Wood (Sally Sayward Barrell), America's first female novelist, was born at York in 1759; York built the continent's first pile bridge in 1761; John Paul Jones's ship *Ranger* was launched at Kittery in 1777. On and on it goes, exponentially increasing as the region is studied and explored.

Though occasionally interrupted by hills, this region is primarily composed of gently rolling terrain, with significant acreage in marsh and swamp. While the shoreline does have many small points and bites, with the exceptions of Brave Boat Harbor, York, Cape Neddick, the Wabhannet River, Cape Arundel and Cape Porpoise Harbors, they are not especially dramatic. There are small fishing fleets along here, but none are especially significant until you get to Cape Porpoise—the only really "deep water" port in the area, and Kennebunkport, which, while relatively shallow, hosts a large pleasure fleet owing to its excellent protection and boatyard facilities. Where the area shines is at its marvelous pure sand beaches There are dozens, including the very popular and famous ones at York, Ogunquit, Moody, and Wells, all of which host large cottage communities. These are strictly seasonable, and the differences they show between high summer and deep winter are startling and dramatic. From the Fourth of July until Labor Day, it is a scene of family fun and get-togethers—towels drying on the line; lost Frisbees and found ones. Along the great beaches you see the blossoming of youthful love, suntan oil by the drumful, and a thousand radios blaring out different songs. All *is* excess in the semi-nude world of summer beach.

In winter, these clapboard cottages that go on for mile after mile seem framed in a poignant loneliness. Where once before one's parking place was defended on pain of irate tirade, in winter no traffic is to be seen anywhere—perhaps a police cruiser, or now and again a dog-walker, a solitary scuffler of ice-crusted sand contemplating matters of heart, employment, and state. It is a boarded-up world—the water and lights turned off, the sea washing in and out in the disturbed vicissitudes of the season, utterly stark.

They are, of course, fragile communities, built on the sand of biblical warning. These places are no more than sand berms, the product of "once-a-century" storms. Behind them are salt marshes, with miles of meandering creeks and life-filled muds, giving nurture to the sea's life beyond. Here the studious or adventuresome summer kid has an alternative to the frenzy of skin, sand and sun at the beach—a view into the stuff of natural history along these shores.

The shore itself becomes considerably more complicated from Cape Arundel eastward, with more coves and peninsulas. Island structures begin, and distances between significant features are shorter. Arundel is, of course, very famous and beloved in the Mainer's heart for the fictional characters that deceased novelist and lifetime resident of Arundel, Kenneth Roberts, placed here. And, where the highways and byways of the coast are generally strip-developed up to Kennebunkport, it is at this charming town that the pattern changes, almost as if it were a dead end. Here a tight cluster of boutiques and galleries are set in a veritable museum of Georgian architecture. As in Kittery and York

The Nubble Lighthouse at Cape Neddick at dawn **right**. Such lighthouses, located as they are against a backdrop of other lighting along the shore, are critical to the lives of inshore craft and vessels. The light *has* to be distinct!

Dutch-hip and cape-styled homes **center** find themselves waterfront neighbors in the charming and ancient village of York, Maine. Off the beach a downeast-styled lobsterboat, rigged for tuna and swordfishing (both harpoon fisheries), awaits its end-of-season duties.

villages to the West, you know instinctively that living here must convey to the resident a profound and justified smugness!

Biddeford

As we approach the Biddeford area, we find another kind of historical and economic nexus, which exists in a more subdued way at many points along the Maine coast but which is here writ larger, and more plain. Biddeford itself has always been a factory-industrial town, right from its inception. And Biddeford Pool and the adjacent Fortune's Rocks have always been summer recreational areas. But they were once separate entities; the industrialists and their workers ensconced inland and the train-delivered rusticators were isolated from them at the grand inns by the shore. Today they have become the same economic entity, for where once vast spaces presented themselves along the shore for the rider, yachtsman, artist and *bon vivant* from away, now expensive homes of industrialists and professionals are set cheek-by-jowl all along the formerly expansive and inviting shoreline. This is not only a function of the automobile but also of changing values. In earlier times landsmen perceived the sea to be another way of life, actually an alien one, no matter how dependent they were on it for transport. Established people once separated themselves not only from the source of their wealth (factories) but also from the elements and searoads over which their resources and goods flowed. So, where once genteel society clustered together in elegant and fashionable inland neighborhoods (including the sea captains' communities we will discuss later), today the seashore and highly eclectic dwellings give the primary status to this region's can-do business community. Whether they derive their wealth from the great factories in Biddeford or beyond in South Portland, Portland, or the industrial back-of-beyonds inland from there, Biddeford Pool's people for good or ill reflect a new kind of elite Maine lifestyle. Shoreline property has become enormously valuable along the coast, with annual valuations doubling every few years. The name Fortune's Rocks may be taken quite literally on this exemplary stretch of westerly shore.

Across the Saco River from "the Pool" exists the longest uninterrupted stretch of sand beach in the state and the only *carnival* community along the shore—Old Orchard Beach. Where the other well-known recreational

The Brick Store Museum in Kennebunk, **left**, housed in a storefront building dating back to 1825, has constantly changing exhibits of both Maine history and of contemporary art.

beaches are primarily seasonal-cottager communities, Old Orchard pulls out all the stops to be the *sine qua non* itinerant vacationers' seashore, complete with fairway and carnival attractions, rides, gewgaws, hawkers, boardwalk, and sugar in every form a parent can fear or imagine. For reasons of geology as well as climate, Old Orchard has become a favorite summer vacation spot for French-speaking Canadians, and so most of the business here is bilingual, as is the dating behavior. Maine has many of its own versions of fun, but here it takes off its clothes and does it *their* way. Generally, natal Maine first-time visitors simply cannot believe it, but here it is, and whoopy!

Upstream of the Saco River mouth, back of Biddeford and its factories and out onto the plains of its relatively vast watershed, we find an area in which another historical drama was largely played, for here were once the great pinelands of such concern to the British Admiralty in late colonial times.

Saco Bay itself, whose waters oversee the panoply of fun at Old Orchard Beach, is yet another cradle of historically early settlement and economic activity. At 90 degree angles off of fashionable Prouts Neck (FDR made a point of officially eliminating the many apostrophes from all Maine coast nominal designations; he thought them to be a bother), lie historic Richmond and Stratton Islands. Stratton was an early *independent* trade station. In 1630 John Stratton, its first settler, traded muskets, powder and shot to the local Indians for furs. These in turn sold in England for his own supplies and sterling for investment. Such independents were a thorn to the officially sanctioned mainland settlements, which were obliged to increase and fortify their communities in order to maintain their licences to trade—a nicety forgone by independents like Stratton.

## Pine Trees and Politics

The Saco drainage area, from the coast to the "back of beyond," stretching out across the south-central flatlands, was *the* classical pinelands of the notorious King's Broad Arrow disputes over the disposition of mast-stock. These disputes became one of the primary bones of contention with the English, leading to the American Revolution. The American school textbook version, with which most readers will be at least vaguely familiar, is that all North American white pines over 22 inches in diameter "at breast height" belonged to the English Crown. Though this dispute had tremendous ramifications, the details of it are not well known and the statistics of it are singularly *not* impressive. The whole issue was a true scandal, on the one hand, and a tempest in a teapot, on the other hand.

First, it is not generally understood *why* the American forest resource had become so important to Great Britain. There were two

A windjammer cruise ship **center** sits to her anchor, waiting for the wind a light summer frontal system will likely bring. Coastal people are weatherwise, and know that things will not be the same for long.

reasons. First were the technological improvements that had been made in ordnance—guns, during the mid-late eighteenth century. The coking of coal had made larger and more reliable casting of cannon possible, and so the obvious and necessary naval response was to produce larger ships to carry the larger guns, and to resist the onslaught of the similarly larger ordnance in enemy hands. Ships, of course, were made of wood, and so the manpower and resource implications followed the naval requirements. Bigger and more effective guns meant bigger and more effective ships, manned by more and better-trained sailors. It also meant more manpower was needed in the shipyards to convert more wood into these ships! Look at a few of the statistics (from Albion's masterful book on the subject).

The workhorse ships of the English Royal Navy were the so-called third-raters, 74-gun ships which, with gun decks 168 feet long and beams 47 feet wide, displaced 1,600 tons. On first construction, one of these ships used all the timber from 2,000 oak trees, which, in a mature oak forest, is all the timber growing on 50 acres of forested land. This timber does not count the wood for spars or 30,000 tree nails— the wooden pegs with which ships were fastened—or the prodigious amount of charcoal used to manufacture and forge the ship's metalwork.

An idea of the increment with which wood's use increased during this period can be evoked by comparing two royal timber surveys and then considering the wood-use quantities from two years in the late eighteenth century. Bear in mind that His Majesty's wood was measured in so-called "loads," each of which was 50 cubic feet in dimension. Today we often measure wood in tons, a ton being 40 cubic feet, more or less. So a "load" is a ton plus 25 percent.

Now then, in the survey for 1608, the time of Elizabeth and Shakespeare, the six Crown forests contained 234,000 loads of timber suitable for the Royal Navy. The survey for 1783, 175 years after the earlier one, showed only 50,000 loads to be available in the same forests. That same year, the combined timber use for both merchant and naval construction was 50,000 loads, the *same* figure. They used in one year what was standing. But here is the crunch: in 1791, only eight years later, the merchant yards used 167,000 loads and the

Navy 217,000 loads—totalling 384,000 loads of shipgrade wood—just for the primary construction of ships for that year!

Remember that, although these timbers went into the ship during construction, most of the vessels left the building yard already decaying with rot. The repairs required on them were extensive and continuous, battle damages notwithstanding. The wooden ships, so ably sailed by the iron men of poetry, were voracious gobblers of wood. To service them, the British did two things: they secured their New England colonies from the French, and, as did the Germans, established forest conservation and management as a state practice.

In any case, the English had, quite literally, run out of wood. And Sweden, the usual previous source of their traded wood, went to war and closed off its once-reliable access to shipstock, especially spar-stock—the flawless virgin pine and spruce trees necessary for strong and reliable masts, yards, and booms that all ships require to properly carry sail in all conditions of weather and warfare. The American colonies had plenty of wood, and the British Admiralty determined to lock it up for the exclusive use of the Royal Navy.

Now, it is very important to remember here that all Americans then were Englishmen by government if not by birth. Remember, too, that the revolutionaries, of soon but nevertheless later times, were treasonous criminals from the viewpoint of proper and respectable citizens of the New World colonies. So while many people in the colonies were disgruntled about English negligence of civil intelligence in the colonies, most people towed the various administrative lines necessary to their advantage and English patriotism. Among these requirements was the extremely difficult position of knowing as a good English person how much extraordinary wood resource existed in the nearby backcountry, and yet having to give lip-service to the laws which forbade the exploitation of trees over 22 inches in diameter for civil uses. Like many of us today, our forbearers saw the administration to be respectable enough, but also unrealistic, if not actually crazy sometimes. So everyone in the timber business cheated, and those not in it turned their backs.

Under the Royal Governors, the Royal Foresters tramped their ways through the relatively open pinelands of the Saco drainage

It took 2000 **oak trees** to construct just one 'third-rater' ship of the Royal Navy . . . the 74-gun workhorses of the time.

**Above** Looking down on Portland Head Light, as it looks vigilantly out across the open Atlantic and the mouth of Casco Bay. South Portland and Portland are in the background.

**Below** Maritime winters are bitterly cold—but the landscape is often breathtakingly beautiful.

interior areas within reasonable reach of the riverine systems, and chopped an inverted "V", that is to say, a "Λ", in large prominent view through the bark of all trees deemed to be appropriate for His Majesty's mast-stock.

Such trees had to be of virgin growth, straight, and clear of visible branch growth to a height in proportion to its relative breast-height diamter. A 22-inch tree would have to be clear to a height of, say, 46 feet. A 54-inch tree, the largest of which we have delivery record, was clear to a height of 110 feet! These were impressive trees!

But there were many of these trees, scads of them! In the entire period of this law, fewer than 5,000 of these logs were delivered to the Royal Navy. Indeed, the records of American domestic export of clear sawed woodstock, in the forms of boards, clapboards, deals, flitches, staves, and other odd wood product forms exceeds the Royal Navy deliveries by something on the order of 1:1000, board-foot for board-foot. Cheating was not so much cheating, as it was business-as-usual, quite simply because any other way of doing business was madness. The trees were there, the means of identifying and protecting the resource entirely inadequate and often non-existent (a couple of the Royal Foresters never even left Boston!), and the American pioneer woodsmen, sawyers, and traders were all over the place, very much in business. So, 99 percent of the King's Broad Arrow Pines ended up as boards and clapboards in American homes, and, even more commonly, abroad trading vessels headed to the Caribbean islands. No sawn-stock, of course, was more than 22 inches in width, and owners of pre-revolutionary New England homes today will inevitably show visitors their lovely "pumpkin pine" structural members of impressive dimensions that, in fact, represent half or less of the dimensions of the original tree source!

The point is that the Saco Basin was the focus of most of this hulabaloo. The issue reached into the White Mountains and other New England outer reaches, but the crux of it, as indicated by four decades of Royal Makers and Inspectors in the area, occurred inshore and behind this first of Maine's many bays.

## Richmond and Cape Elizabeth

Nearby Richmond has a more complex history. The great French explorer Samuel de Champlain had attempted to establish a permanent settlement on an island in the mouth of the Saint Croix River, a complete disaster for all concerned. Like many European newcomers of the early period (and today,

still!), the explorers grievously underestimated the severity of North American winters, confusing latitudes, with which they were familiar, with great continental air currents, to which they were complete strangers. The following year Champlain cruised up the Maine coast, landing at various places, including Richmond Island. He was deeply impressed, reporting "fine oaks and nut trees, the soil cleared up, and many vineyards bearing beautiful grapes in their season." For this reason he named the place "Isle of Bacchus." Yet for some unknown reason, Champlain declined to set down roots on Richmond, and

eventually he chose the shores of the Bay of Fundy for his Acadian headquarters. Later, Richmond, too, became a trading station, but a much more significant one than nearby Stratton, for by the mid-seventeenth century, 60 men were employed at fishing and converting pine and oak into clapboards and staves. Today, both islands are wild again, their soils awaiting the archaeologist's trowel.

Ashore from Richmond lies Cape Elizabeth, today an attractive and wealthy bedroom community to nearby Portland. Graced by famous Portland Head Light, the oldest lighthouse in America (built in 1791 on the orders of President George Washington), and Two Lights State Park, this gateway to the first of Maine's great bays is one of the most frequented, and certainly photographed, places along the coast of Maine.

## Seasons and the Coastal Landscape

In those extraordinary days of the Watergate scandal, just following the so-called "Saturday Night Massacre", just-fired investigator Archibald Cox was asked by the press what his plans were, now that his services had been dismissed. He replied, "I'm going back to the coast of Maine!"

Home is home for everybody, and everybody obviously loves to get back there once other places have palled, for whatever reason. Home is home. But there are, here and there on the planet, places that truly beckon, and it is no wonder that even seasonal residents of the Maine coast feel like they come home, in the deepest sense of the word, when they return to these shores. Residents of this region are not so much loyal *to* it as organically compelled, indeed fixated *by* it. To be sure, all parts of the nation have this quality for some of its residents, but the Maine shores score a ten out of ten in this regard.

The most likely reason is that this mix of landscape, seascape, and seasonal round somehow conspire to create a sense of time that differs from the host culture. Mainers have a difficult time in believing in *destiny*.

The island autumn
season, **above and right**, is
more subdued than that on the mainland, less
glamorous and brilliant. But
islanders will tell you that it *glows* more.

Destiny implies a linear sense of history—that things just move on from one thing to another. This compels a very opportunistic way of dealing with life. The Maine maritime sensibility is more prone to believe in fate than destiny and to concentrate its attentions on the *cycles* of life rather than on the ever-changing. New times and events are generally seen to be simply the old in new dress. There is a tendency to wonder what all the rush and hoopla is about among visitors, in the cities east of Maine, and on the television set. If not all Mainers believe that it's all a bunch of damn nonsense, certainly many of them refuse to give it all the credit it seems to solicit. Lots of people who move to these parts do so because they find this attitude very sensible and attractive.

The sea and meteorology of the region do not fool around, and soundly humiliate any person's presumptuous and impatient attitude toward it. And the landscape offers such variety and seasonal round of attractions and activities, that to *wait until the time is right* becomes a pleasant habit for the local, no matter how frustrating to the visiting can-do, ambitious, let's-get-on-with-it visitor or maladjusted transplant. Nature tells people what to do and when, but you have to listen; a time to build and repair, plant and harvest, pile and burn, hunt and nurture, and so on—the whole ball of Ecclesiastical wax! Maine people just don't rush when asked to and stop altogether when ordered to. They know a fool when they see or hear one!

Being part of northern New England, the Maine coast has all the famous features that the designation implies, but the proximity of the ocean delays and modifies the usual schedule. Spring, when it comes at all, comes late. It's a standard joke that "last year spring was on a Thursday." The winter-chilled sea is very slow to give up its grip on shoreside temperatures. On the other hand, autumn and early winter are delayed as well. Coastal gardeners just love to talk to inlanders and brag about their still-viable tomatoes in late October—some years, into late November—though they won't mention the plastic covering . . .

This is still the land of the bean supper in the church vestry, of the Sunday drive, and spontaneous open house. Somehow, the urge to go "cruising" as a youth never abates around here, and the would-be lovers lanes and "parking places" here welcome and host people of almost all ages and social status almost any time. People just like to get out and around to watch their world go through its endless, familiar, comfortable, beautiful cycles.

It is, of course, an outdoor sportsman's paradise, and no surprise that every major town, and some small ones, have successful outfitters in their chambers of commerce. Most households sport firearms and fishing tackle set, cleaned, oiled, and ready; canoes, cross-county skis, snowmobiles, and ATVs abound in yards and garages all along the coast. And any room with a dozen local people will yield a rock house, a wild-flower buff, a bird-watcher, and seashell collector. Whether it is by hunting and fishing, or binoculars and camera, or walking, skiing or just staring out to sea, coastal people are intimately connected with their natural environment.

**Seashell collecting** . . . big ones, colored ones, strange shaped ones . . . a paradise for shell collectors.

# Yachting and Boating

Certainly one of the most distinctive aspects of any coastal village or town is its harbor, and of its harbor, its boats. As mentioned earlier, it was always access to water transport that originally gave these townships their virtual reason-to-be. Boats and shipping were, and in some senses remain, central to coastal existence, compromised though they may be these days by the economic power of modern terrestrial transportation systems. But even though goods and services generally no longer arrive by sea, it is still from the sea, that these towns derive their spirit and identity. Community pride will more likely yield bragging about its dozen or so commercial fishermen than about its large factory or trucking firm—no matter how much the economic realities would have it otherwise. The maritime self-image of man-and-the-sea, its self-reliance, its *ableness* and dangers, constitute a kind of folk religion.

This maritime sensibility has always been enormously attractive to pleasure boatmen, and since the 1920s an ever-increasing number of east coast yachtsmen have made the coast of Maine a goal, a mecca and center for their sport. Even before that, the rusticators in centers like Falmouth, Biddeford Pool, Boothbay, Dark Harbor, Camden, North Haven, and Northeast Harbor established yacht clubs and active programs in sailing education and class sailboat racing. Indeed, the "North Haven Dinghy" is the oldest class racing boat type still racing in the nation (from 1884!). But it was the coast of Maine *as a goal* in the sailor's breast that gave the area its true mystique. Before radios, electronic navigation, and depth-sounding devices, this area of strong tidal currents, many rocks and ledges, and surprise dense fogs gave the cruising navigator from Boston or New York a real challenge and thrill. Today, even with these modern conveniences, the relatively new sailor asks himself, "Am I ready, yet, for Maine?" And the first cruise downeast constitutes a genuine adventure for everyone who first attempts it.

**Left** When they think about the obvious harshness of downeast maritime winters, visitors often ask what year-round residents do during these times of short days and long cold nights. Well, sometimes they go iceboating, or perhaps touch off a Christmas rocket.

A day out in a windjammer, perhaps
in the *Lewis R French* **left** out of the North End Shipyard
at Rockland, is a must for visitors
to Maine, where even in summer fogs **above right** may
make warm clothing essential. *Victory
Chimes* **above** is unique in having three masts; boats of
all sizes, however, take part in the
annual Windjammer Days race, seen **below** at the point
where it passes Browns Head Lighthouse
**below right**.

# I N D J A M M E R

Once smitten by these waters, there is no going back for the usual yachtsmen. Many cruising families do take their boats home each fall, but more and more the pleasure boatman simply leaves his craft in Maine, to be landed each spring in the waters he's bound to prefer, once experienced. Where only a decade ago a small village boatyard, on any harbor worthy of the designation, handled small workboats only, yachts begin to predominate in the spring round of "fitting-out". And no wonder. As the rest of the East Coast chokes on its pleasure-boat traffic and is stifled in its lack of sufficient marina and yard facilities, (not to mention uncrowded places to go!), Maine's thousands of little bights, coves, tickles, and bays beckon the urban-weary yachtsman. A lifetime of regular and disciplined cruising could never even dent the extraordinary inventory of anchorages.

The traditionally great yachting centers remain so, but as the number and kinds of seasonal residents increase, the dominance of these centers has been much diminished. All up and down the coast, yachts bob at their moorings, and few summer horizons do not sport at least one sail off in the distance. Not that *sail* is the be-all and end-all. Powerboats of every shape and description abound, but, there is a different emphasis on powerboats in Maine. The waters, after all, are chill, and so the "pleasure wagons" and high performance craft, common to the westward, are relatively few. Most pleasure powercraft in Maine are practicality-oriented, used for fishing or simply cruising about to explore inshore sights, bird-and-seal-watching, or just being on the water. Though the great yacht clubs of the Northeast now regularly plan their racing-cruising schedules to include Maine, and the descendants of rusticators still race and tipple out of their traditional harbors, it is the ordinary boatman who now claims the coast as his own, and whose children rub shoulders with the year-round kids in a great coast-long fleet of small sailing craft and outboards.

The salt-bank schooner and trading vessel of yesteryear is no longer discharging or taking-on cargo down at the wharf. But there are the windjammers "making-out-by", dozens of new moorings being set down each year, and there is not a person in town who does not cast a glance over the fleet, and out to sea, with feeling and attachment.

# PORTLAND HEAD TO SMALL POINT AND CASCO BAY

The Casco Bay region has some ironic qualities. On one hand, it is in many ways the commercial and cultural center of the state—the place one goes for the best professional services, educational opportunities, access to markets, and that thing you need but is not available elsewhere east of Boston. On the other hand, and partly for the same reasons, people from the rest of Maine, and certainly along the coast, regard Casco Bay and its dominant city of Portland to be rather alien to the essential heart-throb of what is usually thought to be *Maineness.* The reasons for this are not easy to identify. True, it is highly populated and commercially diverse and active, but there are other densely populated and commercially vital places in the state. In addition, there are other ethnically varied urban areas, and professional talent is generally available around Maine, if not so concentrated as here. No, it is something else—perhaps a general cosmopolitanism, but more likely a general sense that the region's critical mass of citizenry has turned its face to the world, rather than inward, as is often the inclination of the rest of the coastal populus.

*Portland*

Though it is possible to walk from one end of downtown Portland to the other in half an hour, and through Falmouth, Yarmouth, Freeport, and Brunswick in minutes, there is in these towns a sense of people not only on the move, but on the make. Eyes are toward the future, not the past; the present is to be grasped and used, and to stop is to fall behind. Politics are those of initiation rather than limitation, and all this seems contrary to the more rural and fundamental habits of mind and action that generally prevail in other Maine coastal areas. While there are pockets of traditional lifestyles and attitudes in the region, they are becoming ever-more isolated and curious to the surrounding frenzy of growth and change. This, of course, is from the outside, looking in.

From the inside, it is all exciting and upwardly mobile. The languid pace and Depression grime that hung on Portland into the sixties is now utterly of the past. Community pride and revitalization are rampant. Professional people from all over the nation have discovered, by word of mouth and business association, that they can halve their salaries from major metropolitan areas elsewhere and yet live better—freer, safer, more healthfully and more productively, and in a friendlier atmosphere here than in the ostensibly weightier hubs from which they've come. Services are complete and superb, yet a ten-minute ride by auto has you out and away in Maine, on the coast or to the mountains, beautiful country, in either case. Here is sin and greed, the symphony and theater, rock concerts and topless joints, greasy spoons and elegant cuisine, erudite lectures and competent consulting, great art and drunks sleeping in doorways; in short, a real live city.

Portland itself is not only a growing and vital city, it is an indomitable one, for it has been virtually destroyed three times. First called by the Indian name Machigonne, then Casco, then Falmouth (a name it held for 128 years), it became Portland on July 4, 1786. Looking closely at the city's logo, you will see a phoenix, for the very appropriate reason that the town has been burned completely flat three separate times, at roughly hundred-year intervals, and thoroughly rebuilt itself to renewed prosperity each time. The first devastation occurred in 1676 when the local

Row after row of seasonal cottages, inns and shops line parts of the Casco Bay shoreline **right**.

The evolution of Maine folk architecture is evident in this Cushing farmhouse **opposite**. As family size and prosperity increased, ells and wings were added and sheds expanded into barns.

**30**

The **First Parish Church** in Portland was built in 1826. Its essentially conservative design is enlivened by detail in wood and granite.

Indians, allies to others fighting the King Phillip's War centered in Massachusetts, assembled at their summer encampment place on Peak's Island and from there raided the mainland white community, virtually eliminating it and any further attempts at resettlement for the ensuing forty years. Indeed, the only viable white establishments around or in Casco Bay at the time and a generation after were on good but nevertheless less desirable Casco islands, such as Mackworth, Sebascodegan, Orrs, Bailey, Lower Goose and Moshier. At these places the whites could be contained and their trade kept available, as opposed to either the possible expansive grounds on the mainland or the most desirable and productive islands, mostly because of good springwater such as Peaks, Great Diamond, Long, and Chebeague, which the Indians kept for themselves. They did this for as long as their health, numbers and navy (they were excellent sailors and pirates) allowed them their hegemony into the mid-eighteenth century.

Later, and after the town of Falmouth had had more than half a century to recoup, its citizens had the spunk, and perhaps ill-considered audacity, to briefly detain Captain Henry Mowatt, of His Majesty's Royal Navy, in 1775 as a protest against the Crown. This indiscretion cost the town almost its entire self. Again it was burned flat, but the event inflamed more than the city, sparking outrage and revolutionary fervor throughout the colonies. It may have been "just one more thing," but another thing it most certainly was, and the citizens began rebuilding immediately, in any case.

History proceeded in its illimitable way, at double time considering the importance of Portland's ideal location by protected deep water so near to the open sea. The year 1819 found here the constitutional convention that would, the next year, separate Maine from Massachusetts, and for the next seven years the town would be the new state's new capitol. But on July 4, 1866, Portland again burned utterly to the ground, leaving the entire population homeless, though no lives were lost. Consequently, Portland today boasts colonial dwellings only about its periphery, and Victorian ones only here and there, and these are late, if splendid. Basically, the inner city must be described as turn-of-the-century to Wil-

sonian, but this is no reason to gnash one's teeth in architectural horror, as this town's true bravado comes subtly. Its famous and significant buildings (Longfellow House, Sweat, Victoria, Tate, and Neal-Dow houses), are all just gilding to a more consistently intriguing feature—namely, the extraordinary number of stain-glass windows that are common to the entire town. There are thousands, and "window-cruising" constitutes a hobby for many a Portlander.

In any event, Portland today is hot stuff. The old Port Exchange District has been built up in a decade, and what run-down places can yet be found are thought to be opportunities

Keeping watch over the mouth of Casca Bay, Halfway Rock **above** marks its place between Cape Elizabeth and Small Point.

In some ways, Casco Bay **below** reminds observers of Cape Cod, or even the Jery Shore, but residences here know different.

rather than eyesores. Portland is, quite simply, jumping. And the surrounding region is following suit with equal energy. Indeed, it is thought by professional demographers that the twenty-first century will see the Freeport-Richmond axis, up the river systems half-way to Gardiner and the Augusta-dominated Kennebec tidal headwaters, as the future population hub of the state. These predictions have not been ignored by realtors!

## Falmouth, Yarmouth and Freeport

Meanwhile, we wend our way west and north about Casco Bay through interesting country and fine small towns and communities. Falmouth, which inherited Portland's old name, is today a seaside suburb of the city. It is known among nonresidents primarily for the village of Falmouth Foreside and its large, all-service yacht marina and very elegant shore-side homes—remarks which extend to the ensuing towns of Yarmouth and Freeport as well. These (formerly) shipbuilding towns are thoroughly imbued with domestic pleasantness, and their contemporary designations as "bedroom towns" ignore the many small institutions and businesses that are everywhere underway in them. Freeport is well known to otherwise passersby for the L.L. Bean Company, famous outfitters since 1911, when its founder invented the peripatetic Maine Hunting Shoe, considered by many to be mandatory footwear in the autumn fields. Another, much more odd attraction to the township is the so-called "Desert of Maine," which by reputation "suddenly appeared" over a hundred years ago on ostensibly fertile farmland. Canny old-timers, however, will say when pressed that the farm was severely overgrazed by sheep. Whatever, these shifting dunes have buried trees over 70 feet high and provide a spectacle otherwise unheard of east of Cape Cod. Finally, old Jameson's Tavern, established at Freeport in 1779, is reputed to be the place at which Maine's separation papers from Massachusetts were signed in 1819.

## Brunswick

Originally devoted to lumber-milling and ship-building, Brunswick very early on switched to textiles and other factors, leading the way for the rest of New England's industrialization. Maine's first cotton mill was set up here in 1809, and wheels whirled away into the present day. Bowdoin College calls this home too, and from its first academic year in 1802, it has provide first-rate higher education to its undergraduates, who have counted among their number many later-distinguished names—Longfellow, Hawthorne, Perry, Pierce, Hamlin, and many others.

## The Harpswells

South of Brunswick lie the amazing Harpswells, all subsumed under the township of Harpswell, but to its residents really an affiliated cluster of eight difference communities and 45 separate islands. This is a land of bridges and spectacular ocean views, for a more broken-up and fragmented terrain could not be requested. A glance at a map, chart, or aerial photograph is a veritable lesson in the glacial origin of this topography—great points, peninsulas of land reaching out into Casco Bay, hosting miles of seasonal and year-round homes and splendid recreational boating, all in a parallel sweep of geomorphology. The surrounding islands make up the northern component of the Casco archipelago, which for a couple of generations were known as the "calendar islands," after the belief that there was one for each day of the year, less one for leap years. Alas, some spoilsport actually got around to counting them, finding only 222, a nice number in its own right, but a calendar for some other planet.

Here we must back up slightly, return to Brunswick, and move briefly up the Andros-

Scores of Victoria and
Georgian-styled homes grace the lovely
village of Kennebunkport.

One of York's many classic ell-and-wing farmsteads **center**, along with one of the township's old fireman's coaches in perfectly restored order.

coggin River whose hydropower was always the reason-to-be for Brunswick's industrial base), and come to Merrymeeting Bay, a broad diversionary estuary where, briefly, the Kennebec River loses its concentration and expands only to be split back into itself and the Androscoggin. Downriver on the Kennebec we will find Bath in the next chapter, but here in Merrymeeting Bay lies one of the most important stopovers for migratory birds on the Eastern Flyway. The bay is always lovely, a nesting site for raptorial birds (including the American Bald Eagle), and popular sightseeing grounds for colonial home buffs, but far and away its glory are the tens of thousands of ducks and geese which biannually stop here to "top off their tanks" for their migratory ardor. Sportsmen converge on the place in droves, as does the binoculars set, each suspecting the other of subversion; both groups bask in the sheer excess of the avian multitudes.

## Architecture and Community Design

We've mentioned a couple of community design features—for example, the westerly coastal villages look the way they do because they were marketing and distribution centers for resources and goods located by protected navigable water. But, like so many generalities, this is too broad a remark to provide a picture of what it is that makes these coastal places so special. For every village is unique, reflecting not only the natural variation in terrain and site characteristics of the place but also reflecting particular periods in history, economic specializations, and often distinctive class and ethnic tastes and preferences that have left their mark, even though these no longer apply to present occupants. Towns did tend to specialize; shipbuilding towns differed in dwelling, character, and community layout from mill towns, fishing towns, shipping towns and so on. Finally, journeymen carpentry once tended to be an itinerant trade, and these craftsmen would bring architectural styles typical of faraway places to their new work on

the Maine coast.

More than a few books have been devoted to New England homes, but a few coastal notes on the subject belong here.

Metropolitan places in Maine exist in the same way and for the same reasons as others nationwide. Their original form and character have been largely swallowed up by the exigen-

industrial towns, such as Biddeford, Brunswick, Rockland, Belfast, and Ellsworth are all likewise experiencing renewed vigor and self-appreciation. Traditional Yankee values of dexterity and manual competence are combining with contemporary commercial instincts not only to invest in and speculate on the economic future of real estate but also to seek renewed roots in community pride and neighborhood revitalization. Old towns are being made new again, and refusing to remain embarrassed about their enterprising pasts, whether in manufacturing, warehousing and shipping, oil depots or whatever.

The smaller towns, with less generalized industry, today show their historic colors more readily. The old homes and churches predominate and are easy to find. What is so remarkable is not just their beauty but also their individuality, their unique character from one town to the next. An educated eye can spot immediately the historical identity of a village's heritage—for example, that the builders in Southport, Bristol and other places along the Damariscotta River came originally from Cape Cod; that Kennebunkport is a veritable museum of Georgian architecture; that the architects of Bar Harbor and Northeast Harbor had been to Newport, Rhode Island, before, and that Thomaston and Searsport sported sea captains who wished the best of their age for their "sea widows" and sprawling, if episodic, families. Likewise, a brief sojourn off the main streets of Wiscasset, Waldoboro, Camden, Belfast and other riverine towns will show the row-house structures that signal a mill-town's heritage. The point is that, by contrast, our modern and rather homogenous economy allows all of the present residents not only to point to community roots, but to *brag* about them. Simply by moving from one room to another in the ways that old structures direct, we, in our own ways on the coast of Maine, reflect a continuity of the past in habit and expectation, even if we are cast in problems and concerns of today and not of those who first built and occupied these dwellings and public structures.

Everyone has his own preferences. Colonial and Cape fans have their visiting places, as do the Victorian and Edwardian admirers. Carpenter Gothic lovers can go crazy in Northport and Belfast, and plain old-fashioned ell-and-wing farmhouse buffs can have a field

The majestic **bald eagle**, with its distinctive white head and tail, has a wingspread of up to eight feet. It lives near rivers and lakes and feeds mainly on fish.

cies of modern commercial life, though some of the old remnants of earlier lifestyles remain and even celebrate revitalization as young professional people discover the latent integrity of heritage structures and neighborhoods. Portland, with its Old Port Exchange district and waterfront redevelopment efforts, is one of the most prominent examples. But smaller

**Overleaf** Acadia National Park's Ocean Drive offers one spectacular vista and natural area after another. **37**

Pure architectural
examples of the Victorian and Georgian
periods, as well as these,
with much addition of carpenter Gothic
filligree in wood, can be
found all along the coast of Maine.

day in all directions. However what is perhaps most impressive and significant architecturally along the byways of the Maine coast is the degree to which personal discrimination and expression is manifest in all the considerations that go into home and building siting and construction. Seldom, if ever, will two houses or buildings be aligned or set-back any way near alike! A hundred or more years later, we can virtually *hear*, or at least imagine, the conversations held and decisions made by couples long dead about the particular way the sun used to shine on the knoll, where the well should be dug and which views would be enjoyed from which rooms. Contrary to the present common philosophy, that collective community design should be made collectively and so produce an overall impression of unity, often with sterile results, Maine coastal communities yield their absolute unity by distinctly uncollective means; by people expressing family and individual requirements in a context of shared, but not coerced, values. Maine coastal dwellings and buildings and village layouts are generally beautiful; exceptions are nearly always the result of insensitive, if not cynical, later additions. If zoning and planning boards of the Maine coast are famous for their conservatism, can anyone visiting from away look at the beauty and integrity of the architecture and wonder why?

## Rusticators and Cottagers

The post-Civil War period brought many changes to American civilization, not the least of which was a moneyed middle-class that lived in cities. Yet the country ethic remained strong in the urban breast. There was a guilt attached to urban capitalism, and this guilt was fueled by the genteel sentiment of the period's literature. The philosophies of Emerson, Thoreau, and Cooper and many others of an earlier generation had influenced people's thinking through the years, and by the 1880s it had become nearly mandatory for respectable mercantile citizens to get out into the country-

side in some way to renew their tarnished spirits. Waiting to serve, and in some ways to help create this luxurious sentiment, were the shiny new railroad and splendid steamboat companies. Mountain, lake, and seashore spas opened up nearly everywhere that was appropriate, and the coast of Maine was no exception.

The whole phenomenon was quite literally a function of the transportation employed. A day-trip by train brought you to the westerly beaches, the last popular stop being Biddeford Pool. Some night travel by train, or overnight by steamboat, would find you in Rockland, there either to stay or more likely to embark on another steamer for points further east, the final one being Bar Harbor. There were dozens of popular destinations, and at all of them, one or more large frame inns would scoop up the itinerant weary and provide the best of food and lodging for them. Great porches and wicker chains, billiards and cards, nature lectures, badminton, croquet, lantern slide shows, hiking trails, small boat sailing and canoeing all awaited the travelers.

Naturally it was not long before these discretionary funds for travel and inns became discretionary moneys for property, and a cottage of one's own. And so the great inn centers became rusticator cottage centers. By *cottage*, we mean here rather large and relatively grand structures by contemporary standards—eight or ten bedrooms not being unusual. They exist in neighborhood pods all along the coast, some of the larger concentrations being at York, Mere Point, and other upper Casco Bay Peninsulas, the ensuing points from there to Boothbay, Cushing, North Haven, Islesboro, Blue Hill, Bar Harbor, and Northeast Harbor. At these places, from the 1890s through the Great Depression, well-to-do families displaced themselves to take in the salt air, to read, to engage their children in genteel sports, and certainly to hobnob with others of like persuasion, however different the cities of origin. But even at that, friends and acquaintances from home were usually one's summer neighbors as well, and different spas tended to specialize in their collection of participants.

Someone, of course, had to tend all these properties, not only to caretake them during the long off-season, but also to service the boats, parties and celebrations of the languid/

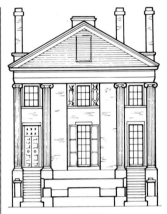

**Charles Clapp House** in Portland was built in 1833, at a time when domestic architecture gained lustre from the handsome granite stone quarried locally.

41

giddy summer season. These were the local coastal people, and cottager-tending became a local industry wherever the lifestyle had sprung up. Without a doubt, there was a strong class distinction applied in these circumstances, yet there was also a mutual respect and appreciation established across the class boundary. Local and summer kids played together, and the local caretakers often became something like surrogate aunts and uncles, even confessors. The ladies could talk sensible girl talk in the kitchen, and the master of the house would come down in the fall to camp out in the great hall, to duck shoot, and to tipple with his Mainer caretaking friend. It was an unspoken bargain, and worked well both ways. Maine winters were never known for their profits shown on the local ledger!

After World War II, things began to change. Yet another class of Americans was emancipated with discretionary funds, and these people, in vastly larger numbers, discovered the attraction of the Maine coast to establish in turn either their own communities of small cottages or to buy up local homes and farm dwellings for recreational purposes. More diverse and generally spread around the shores and through the villages, these business people, teachers and engineers have cast coastal summer society in yet a different light—enthusiastic, participatory, optimistic, though not especially sensitive. Today's usual cottager is much more mobile and infusive than his rusticator forebearer (who still remain behind larger hedges), and their impact on coastal communities has been significant and in some ways traumatic. They want to shop. They want public services. Often, they want changes. And so, today, many coastal communities are taking on a very different character from what once prevailed. Neighborhoods that once resounded in neighborhood life are now boarded up all winter. Public services are overtaxed. And local children, who once naturally looked forward to carrying on local ways of life, now have new behavioral models to turn their heads. Influences that once disappeared on Labor Day now remain in the mind and weaken traditional expectations. The coast of Maine is filled with things and influences from the past, but contemporary history gives them less and less credence.

Tourism is, perhaps, having an even more

**Left** and **center** Bay laurel peeks out of the dome granite, block-faulted cliffs loom and aspen stands eking out a tenuous existence amidst the scrabble and ledges of Acadia National Park.

traumatic effect. The traveler is having even more effect on the texture of Maine coastal summers than seasonal residents through sheer impact of numbers. If you consider that Acadia National Park is fully three-fourths of the distance downeast, and that it alone receives over four million visitors a year, you can capture an approximation about the growing effect on coastal towns. To be sure, most of them strive to get to Mount Desert directly, via the turnpike to Bangor, or along Route One, on which the great peninsulas shoreward along the way are bypassed. But, nevertheless, the tourist facilities being created for them are changing the face of coastal Maine. And the pace of life. Once quiet towns are now a frenzy of activity in summer and nearly cadaverous in winter, as the locals take their summer earnings and themselves become more itinerant.

And so, here and there along the coast, groups of citizens are being formed to revitalize traditional economies, and to diversify the local year-round sources of income. Young professionals are beginning to set up shop. Cottage industries are being established. Value-adding manufacturing and processing plants are being built—all to keep community integrity alive and well against the economic impact of the uncaring transient. The philosophy is, of course, that something so precious and fine as this part of the world is worth keeping and caring for.

# POPHAM TO OWLS HEAD: THE COAST SHOWS HER COLORS

To round Small Point at Phippsburg is to enter another kind of coast, of a sort most yachtsmen, say, think of as having the look and feel of true Maine coast terrain and character. And the same can be said of those who arrive to this region by auto. It's different. Something has changed. Different topographical features, of course, cast their own peculiar aura over an area, and where highly indented land accompanies a major estuary—in this case, the Kennebec River—the resulting region is bound to have much of interest to people. Again, such landscape provides protection, navigable water, the high biological productivity that usually occurs where large rivers drain into the sea, and, in the case of this area, distinct visual prominence from the sea.

For obvious reasons, the early explorers had no charts of these waters—only cursory and often (purposely) vague descriptions by barely literate skippers and explorers, and the semi-drunken pub-room brags of completely illiterate, probably pledged-to-silence fishermen. Exceptions were generally privy (secret) counsel to the various crowns involved in colonial enterprise. In any case, to go aground in these waters was distinctly *no fun*, and so the captains were very loath to be very intrepid about poking into places. The usual practice was to hang off of the coast and seek out prominent points that boded to be very steep, with plenty of deep water right up to the visible land. Once these were spotted and negotiated, the first anchorage possible was used, and the ship's boats then employed to explore the reaches and byways of the area. Consequently, the very earliest habitation sites were on points and islands, and the secondary ones established at the head of easily navigable waters, often at a falls or rapids of some sort, where alewife and salmon runs could be exploited, so long as the Indians behaved themselves. Phippsburg and its Popham Beach area at the mouth of the Kennebec exemplify the early habitation sites, Wiscasset, at the navigable head of the nearby Sheepscot, is a fine example of the secondary ones.

*Popham to Owls Head*

The same year that Jamestown, Virginia was settled, 1607, an English expedition set down roots at Parker Head in Phippsburg. This became known as the Popham Colony. The attempt at settlement ended in disastrous failure through much sickness, a terrible winter and plain bad luck. The colony did manage to construct the first European-designed ship ever built in America, however, the *Virginia*, of 30 tons, built at what is now Popham Beach. Today, Popham Beach is a lovely strand known for its (unusual for Maine) excellent striped-bass surf fishing. And upstream of Popham Beach, at Bath, the second (after fishing) of America's great arts, shipbuilding, goes on today in an intense following of the area's tradition. For 200 years the gentle riverside banks of the Kennebec at Bath have supported the mighty weight of great ships abuilding; in her heyday, the Kennebec saw schooners of up to seven masts and the hardy down-easters that replaced the more romantic, if much less practical, clipper-

So much of New England's, and so America's, past is tied to the quest for religious freedom **right**. Freedom by sapphire sky and intertidal water, this early nineteenth-century church in Phippsburg continues to provide spiritual expression to fifth- and sixth-generation parishioners.

**Opposite** An eclectic lobsterboat in Friendship, Maine sits to her mooring in wait for a host of nautical tasks.

44

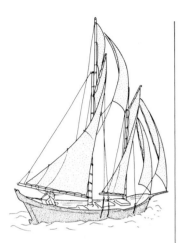

Used originally for the local sardine industry the **Fastport pinky** now makes a popular cruiser for four people.

**Overleaf** A flat-calm summer's day on the waters off Phippsburg township awaits a flat-bottomed skiff, probably a young Mainer's first lobsterboat.

46

ships of the mid-nineteenth century. *Hundreds* of boats were built here, and the tradition lives on today as the Bath Iron Works turns out the best vessels afloat in the modern surface navy, employing 7,000 skilled workers in the process.

## Boat Building Ship Building

It was Maine's fate to become a great center for the building of all manner of seagoing craft. Fishing and the water transport of resources and goods, of course, demanded craft and vessels of many types. But Maine was not unique in this regard; all of colonial America had need of watercraft and built them. It is just that Maine built *more* of them, probably a reflection of its enormous timber supply and its large reserve of skilled craftsmen capable of the work.

Until sound evidence emerges as to a Viking presence in Maine, we can assume that the first boat built by people of European extraction in America was built in Maine: the shallop *Virginia* built at Popham Beach in 1607. The Indians were prolific builders of good boats—not simply the famous small dugouts and bark canoes but large dugout-composite structures as well, large enough for a number of men to venture forth offshore for whales, seal and swordfish, of which there was abundant evidence in their kitchen middens. Indeed, the Indians of these parts showed themselves to be excellent seamen from the earliest times by their enthusiasm and ability to steal and effectively man European and colonial vessels whenever an opportunity presented itself!

Nearly all able white males born on the coast of Maine took part in small boatbuilding, of some sort and to some degree, up into at least a part of the twentieth century. Every village worthy of the designation had at least one full-time boatbuilder, usually several, and everyone who used boats also had to take care of them.

Maine's boatbuilding heritage includes many types of traditional forms—from simple, three-plank, flat-bottomed skiffs through dories, shallops, wherries, peapods, gigs, tenders, dinghies, and punts; to small sloops, yawls, schooners and ketches. There were pinkies and dogbodies, small brigs and brigantines, snows, scows and barges, Johnboats and gondolas. Though varied in form, the basic structure of hardwood framing under softwood planking was common to all of them, and a craftsman of one could and did shift from one to another (with some study and consultation) as economic necessity dictated.

Even though time has passed and introduced changes in the forms of boats preferred—pleasure yachts, outboards, and of course lobstering and fishing boats—the skills required to build and repair them remain the same. Boatyards and small boatbuilding shops dot the Maine coast all along its length; the famous centers of the trade just exemplify locally what is general. Indeed, there is these days a renaissance of wooden boatbuilding underway in Maine, flourishing under the instruction available in the boatbuilding schools and programs in Bath, Rockport, Duck Trap, Brooklin, and Machias, to name just a few. If you are traveling along the coast, a glance out the car window at barns, garages and dooryards will reveal thousands of boat projects underway, from raw construction to the occasional effort at revitalizing an ancient veteran. Habitués of the coast of Maine need boats, and the boats are out there!

And not only of the traditional wood sort either, even if sentiment does give a special aura to the older wooden technologies. Maine is not a nautical backwater. Shops specializing in glass-reinforced-plastic (fiberglass), composite wood-resin, aluminium, and steel craft abound also. Maine's fisheries and other commercial marine enterprises demand boats of all kinds, for various uses and of all relevant materials, and she is able to deliver them. Boatmen from everywhere look to Maine's boatbuilding for genuine value—they know that the work ethic is alive and well here.

The same is true of her shipbuilders. The whole scale of ship construction is so much greater than that for boats that it is an altogether different thing, even though the construction and technology ostensibly appear to be the same. A parallel that illustrates the distinction might be made between cooking for one's family and cooking for an army!

# THE SKILL
# OF THE BOATWRIGHT

The ancient craft of boat-building, with its
precise manual skills, survives in maritime Maine. The techniques
of boat-building — from rowing skiffs and
kayaks **right** to large commercial vessels **above and below left** —
have been learned by more than 100 apprentices
at the Apprenticeshop in Rockport. *Perseverance* **below right** is
the first Prospect Marsh pinky to have been
built for nearly a century.

Here and there along the Maine coast, hulks of old coasting schooners sag and rot in the esturine muds **right**. At Mill Cove, Boothbay, the *Edna McKnight* dotes on another era. Some of her old rails and woodwork now embellish a hotel bar in Bath.

Ships were built at many Maine locations up and down the coast; some of them are famous, like Rockland's clipper yard where the *Red Jacket* was built. Even through the haze of history and thousands of large vessels built at a hundred places, the yards at Kittery, and especially Bath, stand out. The Kittery Navy Yard today specializes in nuclear subs, but its shipbuilding past and traditions stretch back to the very beginning of United States Navy warship construction. Indeed, John Paul Jones' ship, *Ranger* was built there. Bath, too, builds warships today, easily visible as one crosses the bridge over the Kennebec River at Bath. However, where destroyers and frigates come off the ways today, huge vessels of more peaceable mien once regularly first touched water. For a hundred years before ships of battle could call Bath their birthing place, cargo vessels and even a few great yachts summered up here. There is a saying among Navy men today that "you can always tell a Bath ship," (by its reliability and quality of finish). Likewise, mariners of past times always felt that an order for a ship placed at a Bath yard would yield a "good ship ordered," properly built and on time. Bath was famous for them then and is famous for them now.

And what vessels they were! Once the nation's shippers got over their infatuation with high-speed, man-killing, extreme clipper-ships delivering extravagant cargoes and settled down after the Civil War to create a great economic civilization, Bath shipwrights were there, waiting to create and develop the coasting schooners and downeasters that would do the job. These were large, sensible, seagoing ships that carried large amounts of cargo, kept the seas, and required relatively few men to man. Their scheduled burden was for everything! Though the great tonnages were in lumber, wood, coal, lime, and other mass bulky cargo, their assignments included everything society required in all directions between supply and demand.

At Bath, as at other places along the Maine shore, these bottoms were brought together and erected "side by each" along the banks of the Kennebec for a half dozen generations. They were elegant, powerfully built, and massive, their hulls an awesome binding of timber. Plain-stock hardwoods—birch, soft and hard ash and maple, red oak—were combined with the more traditional shipbuilding timber stocks of white and gray oak to fabricate the great keels and keelsons, stem—and stern—works, frames, shelves, clamps, stringers and deck framing of these ships. Over these "futtock–frames" were applied pinestock, usually, but also spruce and even

say, "I'm going to be a boatbuilder when I grow up!"

## George Town, Arrowsic and Woolwich

The townships of Georgetown, Arrowsic, and Woolwich for natural reasons (of proximity) shared in the more notorious history of the towns across the river. For example, Sir William Phipps, the namesake of Phippsburg (a successful treasure hunter in Bermuda, and later Royal Governor of Massachusetts), was born in Woolwich and worked as a young man in the Arrowsic shipyards. But overall this peninsula has been a region of ordinary and parochial domesticity from colonial times, with plot after plot of saltwater farms. These are often tended in modern times by descendants of their founders, even if their present occupants earn their livings commuting to Bath or beyond.

Somewhat to the east of the Kennebec is its sister river, the Sheepscot, which forms the peninsula. The Sheepscot ranges through the same sort of territory, with similarly consistent if demure history, to Montsweag Bay and Maine's only atomic power plant (Maine Yankee, 20 years in operation), and Wiscasset, always popular among Route One travelers for its beautiful homes and picturesque relic schooners languishing in the muds adjacent to the auto bridge. Here too is the state's "worming" center, one of the more interesting of Maine's many secondary fisheries.

Local growing timber like the fast growing **Gray birch** was used along with ash, maple and red oak to erect large sea-going coasters.

cedar when the pine was scarce. There was always timber of some kind available. After all, from the time of launching to demise, the ship was used continuously and so would pay for itself within only a few trips. Most of the vessels, if lucky enough to survive a natural lifetime, lasted 10–15 years before wind, sea, storms, and overloading with undercare took its inevitable toll. There are none of these vessels left save a couple of smaller ones saved by the Windjammer fleet through much searching, rebuilding effort, and nautical stewardship. A few coasting schooner hulks languish in esturine backwaters, most notably at Boothbay and in sight of the Wiscasset Bridge, now a symbol for Wiscasset Village.

Maine's shipbuilding and traffic today differs radically from past times. Medium-sized vessels—fishing draggers and cruise schooners mostly—still aborn at East Boothbay, Friendship and Thomaston, and vessels up to 50 tons can be hauled and serviced at various yards along the shore. The great days of building peaceable ships in Maine are temporarily in abeyance. The tradition primarily lives on in the area of boatbuilding. In Kittery, Kennebunkport, Yarmouth, Falmouth foreside, Friendship, South Thomaston, Belfast, Deer Isle, Vinalhaven, and Beals Island, it is still plausible that a little kid could

## The Sheepscot Region

The Sheepscot River itself is especially well known for the cod grounds a few miles off its

The Maine Yankee Nuclear Power
Plant in Wiscasset is Maine's only nuclear
facility.

South Bristol Island graces the
outer shores of what begins the so-called
Mid-Coast Region.

A Boothbay farm **above** continues old traditions. Most full-time farming along the coast seriously declined after about 1910, but recent years has seen a resurgence in part-time and recreational farming on the part of young professional people and their families.

mouth. Both Boothbay and Southport Island were very early settlements, famous for their excellent fish delivered in proper condition as trade in England. Since we have mentioned this important trade several times before and now find ourselves at its ancient center—adding the great station at Monhegan offshore from here—this is a good place to discuss why the trade was so important in the early days, even if it was so removed from the European market via small ships on an enormous ocean.

## The Importance of the Early Fishing Trade

Just as England was to have severe difficulty in procuring her ship timber during the mid- to latter-eighteenth century, the very early days of New World exploration in the seventeenth century found all the Northern European nations in desperately short supply of *protein* in the peasants' diet. This was attributable to several causes, of which three were most important. First, the terrestrial sources of protein—livestock and game—were almost entirely in the hands of the nobility and gentry. What grains could have supplied the rural population with the missing margin went to estate and war taxes, feeding warriors, their horses and drinking. These were drinking cultures, and producing liquor was a priority. Everything that went into beer also could have gone into bread! Second, the Renaissance brought industrial progress, and this meant that Europeans finally had become more or less immune to the plague diseases that had regularly relieved the continent of a portion of its population and kept the demand for food in check. The Inclosure Acts (kicking people off their rural holdings), urbanization, and rising social expectations all combined to make overpopulation a very general fact. And finally, through a horrendous fluke of historical bad luck and riverine pollution (probably from the tanning trade and Dutch land reclamation projects), the Baltic and North Sea herring fisheries, on which almost all winter peasant protein supplement had depended for

hundreds of years, failed completely, never to recover. Many people today think of "pickled herring" as some sort of Norwegian curiosity on the grocer's condiment shelf; a luxury of sorts. Balderdash! For hundreds of years it was what kept many of our ancestors alive every winter! So, the North Atlantic fishermen were on a vital mission, if for nothing else but to prevent revolutions in the homeland—malnutrition and revolution, of course, being ancient handmaids. There were other North American fishing shoals and banks to exploit, but these off of the Maine coast were dillies, and the least harassed by other nations in competition with England. Even France gave England her leeway as she went for the terrestrial, rather than maritime, gold. Maine was far away, but worth every effort to king and swabby, down the line...

Neither Boothbay nor Southport are especially important fishing centers these days. Boothbay and its environs has become a very popular tourist town, replete with shops and restaurants catering to the tourists' needs and wants. For all that it is a lovely village, and its neighboring communities are very active in boatbuilding and other marine-related trades, including foundrywork and sailmaking.

## Small fishing Villages

At Christmas Cove and the Damariscotta estuary, we begin to find the sort of small genuine fishing villages that will often characterize the rest of our downeast journey. The river itself is essentially *marine* in its water qualities, but the long narrow passage upstream between the townships of Boothbay, Edgecomb and Newcastle on one side of the river, and South Bristol and Damariscotta on the other, has a special intimacy that appeals to many local and visiting boatmen. Here one can poke out for a tiny taste of the open ocean's bracing air and hefty seas but then scurry back upstream to view the relaxing beauty of attractive woods, interspersed with well-proportioned cottages and small

End of day, as a scallop dragger
cruises home "under the loom of the main,"
past island points and shoals.

A harbor scene at Southport **above** sports Maine's perennial coastal photographic badge — lobsterpots in profusion.

The navigation range **middle** between The Cuckolds, off Southport in the Sheepscot estuary.

farms. In South Bristol the visitor will find the Harvey Gamage Shipyard, one of the very finest remaining commercial yards building large wooden vessels (the Hudson River sloop *Clearwater* is one of them), and, in the village of Walpole, the Ira C. Darling Oceanographic Research Center, the University of Maine's facility for marine research and instruction.

But it is Christmas Cove that first captures one's attentions in the estuary. Named by Captain John Smith, who landed here on Christmas Day, 1614, thus snug community has that "Maine thing" about it—small trim houses of highly diverse personality, its neighborhood dominated by the harbor, full of boats that, like as not, earn a living. It is the first taste of what really begins to happen, by sea, around the corner, at Johns Bay, Pemaquid Point, and beyond. A more complete discussion of the Indian relations that made Pemaquid necessary in the first place is worthy of our attention here. For this, we can do no better than go to Philip Conkling's most excellent book on Maine's islands, *Islands in Time* (DownEast Books, 1981):

. . . after this early flurry of activity, it appears that serious island settlement was slow to develop, no doubt because colonists preferred to huddle close to the mainland fort at Pemaquid during the long, sad Indian Wars.

Warfare between the settlers and the Indians may have been inevitable, given the nearly antithetical conceptions of property rights, but the habit of various Englishmen of kidnapping local Indians to show the folks back home certainly did nothing to increase the Indian's trust of whites. In 1605 Weymouth and his crew, after being shown around the islands and the mainland by the local Sheepscots for nearly two months, "suddenly laid hands upon (five) Savages, two canoes with all their bows and arrows." . . . Two of these kidnapped Indians later returned to Maine when Sir John Popham attempted to found a settlement on Georgetown Island, but the treachery continued. Captain Edward Harlow kidnapped three more Indians from Monhegan in 1611, and Thomas Hunt, part of John Smith's expedition in 1614, kidnapped 24 more and sold them as slaves in Spain "for a little gain."

Since the Indian code of law made a whole tribe responsible for the acts of one of its members, the activities of Weymouth, Hunt, and Harlow, among others, set the stage for later terrorist attacks by the Indians on innocent mainland English settlements. In addition, there were indications that some Englishmen intended to make the kidnapping and selling of Indians a regular business. In 1675, after nearly three quarters of a century of increasing hostilities between the mainland farmers and the Indians, the first Indian War broke out.

After the first wave of Indian attacks on isolated farms in 1675, the settlers from Arrowsic and Southport Islands

evacuated to Damariscove and then to Monhegan. For a short time in 1676, Monhegan sheltered virtually the entire population of the District of Maine. During the Indian wars, islands such as Monhegan, as well as Jewell and Cushing in Casco Bay, served as temporary refuges where the settlers retreated to defend themselves.

The end of the first Indian War in 1676 was a distinct victory for the Indians. Every farmhouse between Falmouth and Pemaquid had been burned to the ground; every settler had been killed, captured, or driven away. With peace reestablished, the English settlers could reoccupy their lands, but each planter had to pay the Indians a tribute of a peck of corn. The settlers also promised not to push their land above the tidal waters of the rivers where the Indians were headquartered during the major part of each year. . . .

The first peace soon degenerated into a second war with the Indians, this time with the French actively participating on the Indian side. As the conflict developed, the fighting grew into a war for control of the new continent that had been claimed by both France and England. Pemaquid marked the easternmost stronghold of the English; Mount Desert was the westernmost part of French Acadia. For the next 80 years, everything in between, including the islands, was a war-torn nomansland . . . nearly every farmhouse east of Wells was

From Ram Island light **left** eastward stretches an archipelago which offers the chilled-water sailor a lifetime of beauty and adventure.

Maine's abundant forests furnished the material for many of its early buildings, like this simple, beautifully proportioned church **below** at New Harbor on Pemaquid Peninsula.

Franklin Light **overleaf**, in Musongus Bay, makes up a typical half-day sail passage for a small cruising boat.

destroyed. Even Monhegan was attacked—by a French frigate carrying a force of several hundred Indians.

During the third war, which lasted from 1703 to 1713, Maine lost between a fourth and a third of all her white settlers, but the Indians suffered more. At the end of the declared hostilities, there were no more than perhaps 300 Indian fighting men remaining east of the Kennebec River, and several of the smaller tribes simply ceased to exist . . . With the exception of fishermen and fur traders, white men were nowhere to be seen in the greatest part of the territory. In 1720, for example, there was only one house standing between Georgetown and the St. Croix River, and it was located on Damariscove Island.

A fourth war broke out between 1722 and 1725, and about a third of the remaining Indians were killed or died of starvation. At some point during the long and bitter century of wars, the conflict of terror and blood boiled over into what can only be described as genocide. The Indians, their weakened tribes reduced to a few old men, women, and children, were hunted down like animals. Cut off from the coastal clam flats, their last means of avoiding starvation was their cornfields, and these were systematically laid waste . . . Maine's Indian tribes had largely been exterminated by 1725.

Such historical drama and pathos rather matches the bold splendor of Pemaquid Point itself. From its proud beacon, built in 1827, one sees directly the "high seas" and has no difficulty at all conjuring up the vision in one's mind of the indomitable and stubborn character of the settlers who pioneered this area. Nearby the point, at Pemaquid Beach, the reconstructed Fort William Henry memorial celebrates the adjacent archaeological digs into the original settlement foundations, their hard-won artefacts on display in the memorial building.

Turning north, one comes upon Muscongus Bay. The auto traveler finds the head of these waters at Waldoboro, an industrial community named after one Samuel Waldo, who attracted a large number of German immigrants to this region by claiming that it and its environs were fully developed, very prosperous, and wholly inviting. His victims, of course, found only a few exhausted proto-Yankees battling the wilderness. Nevertheless, many of these Teutons stayed on to settle Waldoboro and nearby Bremen. Their legacy today remains in local surnames. The severe Old German Meetinghouse and the most poignant cemetery in the area also give testimony to human valor in the face of depraved and cynical hoodwinking.

Downstream into the bay itself are some of the most heavily lobster-fished waters in the

The classic "Friendship sloop" originally designed in 1870 is still built today. It is both fast and easy to control.

world. Experienced motorboatmen and sailors alike will all witness the extraordinary density of the gear here—in August so much that you have the impression of being able to walk over the water dry-shod on the colorful bouys. And this is boatbuilding country, too. Generations of Maine Sloop builders simmered up here, at Round Pond, Friendship, Bremen Long Island and other sites, under the great local names of Carter, Morse, and others. This tradition is today celebrated by the Friendship Sloop Society's annual races in late July, covering the Muscongus waters in a glorious "cloud of sail." Though often called "Friendship Sloops," these lovely craft were the working type all along the coast and were called elsewhere "sloopboats" or "Maine sloops." Friendship and vicinity built some of the best and most famous, however, and so have won the designation of the type through sheer energy, devotion, and nautical press. To this very day, a first-class, traditionally built and rigged sloopboat can be ordered and delivered in Friendship, Maine; though the cost has risen somewhat (around 1,000 percent) since the first great ones were built here a hundred years ago!

## The Islands

And now the islands really begin to proliferate. From Hatchet cove in Friendship, round-about and across the mouth of the St. George River and Port Clyde to Owls Head, the mariner passes a hundred islands of diverse and intriguing character. In the midst of them are Allen Island, the site of Weymouth's historic settlement, Eastern Egg Rock—site of a brilliantly rejuvenated puffin colony—and Andrew's Island, for generations a collection site for down-easter's ballast rock, the weighty fill that allowed hundreds of ships on thousands of voyages to sail without cargo to their next landings in safety. Out and beyond, her ferry traffic leaving from Port Clyde, lies grand old Monhegan Island, luxuriating in heritage, affable people, astounding cliff vistas, and a motley summer artist colony.

Puffins at Matinucus Rock **above right**. Using decoys and bird-population management control of competing bird species, biologists are rehabilitating Maine's formerly healthy puffin colonies. For obvious reasons, they are a great favorite among bird-watchers.

In addition to its well-known history in the fisheries, Monhegan **left** today supports a very popular summer artist colony.

Bleached spruce roots **overleaf** and yachts frame Burnt Island Light on a clear northwesterly day.

Port Clyde, at the mouth of the
St. George River, enjoys the pastel lighting so
common to downeast places.
Maine painters often have difficulty
convincing people from elsewhere
that their art really does show it as it is.

In the early 1980s the owner
of Allen Island in Muscongus Bay cleared
seventy acres of trees so that
sheep could be introduced. The wood was
sold as sawlog, pulp and firewood,
here being loaded on to an LCM landing craft
for shipment to Monhegan. Just
visible through the trees stands a large stone
cross commemorating Weymouth's
early settlement of the island.

Like the puffins, Maine's tern populations **above** have been seriously depleted in recent decades. Here terns return to their long-abandoned nesting site at Eastern Egg Rock, after biologists had prepared the site.

In the early 1980s the owner of Allen Island, in Muscongus Bay, determined to rehabilitate the island's agriculture. Seventy acres of reverted woods were cut and sheep **middle** were introduced on to the newly created pasturage.

Originally Fort Williams, Fort McClary Memorial **below** offers relic and reconstructed buildings, bunkers and emplacements from nearly 300 years of conflicts, both actual and anticipated. It is located in Kittery.

## Edgecomb

Two other historical places worth noting are located here on the Sheepscot, at Edgecomb. Fort Edgecomb, built on Davis Island early in the nineteenth century, is today a public park. Its interesting octagonal wood blockhouse is still standing, ready to give the visiting youngster an imagination-tweaking vision of standing ready-to-arms in defense of the river and her people.

There is also a marvelous old (private) dwelling, Marie Antoinette House, currently situated in the Eddy section of North Edgecomb. Originally in the 1830s, the house stood on Westport Island. Why "Marie Antoinette?" Well, it is one of those legends, yet another story completely accepted locally. The story has it that one Captain Stephen Clough, original owner of this house and a friend and frequent visitor to the French Court of Antoinette's time, offered up his ship and home for the Queen's escape. The escape did not come off for Her Majesty, but the good captain got away from France with a boatload of the royal belongings, some of which remain in this

Golden early morning ground
fog illuminates Broad Cove in Cushing, an
area popular among artists.

A retired anchor and windlass
introduce a panorama of Southern Island.
Such terrestrial combinations
of anchor and windlass were once common
along the coast, used by coasting
vessels when they rode out storms in the lee
of islands.

Herring fishermen **left** take up their twine nets at Tenants Harbor. A large powerblock hoists the ten-fathom-deep netting out of the water and into seineboats and dories, where it is "flaked" and made ready for another "set" later on.

house. Occasional visits are permitted by arrangement with the owners.

The presiding river into Muscongus Bay is the St. George. Allowing easy passage for some eight miles between the genteel and distinctly artistic township of Cushing on the west and the more workmanlike towns of St. George and South Thomaston on the eastern shore, this river has seen almost as many new ship bottoms pass over its muds as has the Kennebec out of Bath. Thomaston, at its estuary headwaters, is perhaps the premier old sea captain's town in Maine, for the very good reason that these headwaters have continually produced ships for over 200 years. Entirely unexplored old fortifications line its shores, and place names like Maplejuice Cove make one's head ring. Across the river and down the peninsula on the ocean side, places like Mosquito Harbor, Tenants Harbor, and Spruce Head are serious, out-to-sea fishing communities, interesting and lovely not for some artificial economy but rather for the innate residential integrity they have. It is also in this neighborhood that some of the great granite quarries which built our eastern cities were first opened up a century and a half ago. In any case, whether outside by boat through Two Bush Channel or inside through the Muscle Ridge Channel, the mariner marks Owls Head and its lighthouse, officially entering Penobscot Bay. By car, the landsman passes through Thomaston into Rockland, and again reaches new country.

Two-Bush and Southern Island lighthouses **overleaf** conspire to lead boatmen into and through the Mussel Ridge Channel, between Seal and Rockland Harbors, at Owls Head. Southern Island boasts one of the few remaining triangular bell towers along the coast, unique structures that housed the mechanisms which gave clanging help to mariners in fog and storm. 71

# FISHING AND THE MAINE COAST

The sea bottom of the gulf of Maine is largely drowned continental shelf, rising here and there relatively near to the surface and so making ideal fishing banks and shoals. These combine with Maine's highly indented coastline to offer hundreds of protected anchorages which make the region perfect for small-scale, short-run, fin-fisheries; small boats able to make a day's pay within an hour's run from the home harbor.

It was the fisheries that attracted Europeans to these shores in the first place. Islands such as Richmond, Monhegan, Matinicus, and Allen and mainland places such as Damariscove, St. George, and Pemaquid were all first settled by fishermen very early in the seventeenth century—in every case, the fish were taken within sight of the fishing stations themselves, the product turned into "cor-fish," (whole cod pickled in brine) or split and dried fish, and the fish oils were tried out and rendered into "traine." Such inshore abundance no longer exists, but the old productive bottoms still give up their charge to hundreds of commercial craft and their hard-working crews.

A half-dozen species make up the bulk of fish landed. First and foremost are the *groundfish*—cod, pollock, hake, haddock and cusk. Traditionally, these fish were exploited by two differed kinds of gear. One kind was handlines—single lines terminated by a weighted jig, sometimes with an attendant "tree" of extra hooks, with or without bait—usually without. The other kind of gear was tubtrawls—long groundlines from which are hung hundreds of baited hooks attached to the groundline by three-to-six-foot long ganglings (pronounced *gangions*). Usually, the ones to use this gear were small craft—dories, shallops, peapods, and other traditional types, many of them still popular among pleasure boatmen. When fishing offshore grounds, these smaller craft were tended by larger vessels, a schooner usually, which acted as home base and processing plant for the dory crews. In any case, use of this traditional gear is much reduced in the modern era. Handlining is generally considered to be a recreational sport, even among fishermen. Tubtrawling is mostly limited to semi-recreational halibut runs in early and mid-spring, getting the lobstermen up, out, and on the water to try to earn a few dollars before the lobsters really

strike, and to dispel the gloom of late winter cabin fever.

## Draggers

Far and away, most groundfish today are taken by draggers and gillnetters. Draggers are relatively large vessels, for the most part, and work out of primary harbors such as Portland, Boothbay, Rockland, and Stonington, where major handling and trucking terminals await the volume of catch. The gear used to "drag" for fish takes considerable skill and experience to use successfully. It is composed of two very stout "doors" which, by the effect of water pressure created by the moving boat, hold open large yawning "wings" and "belly" nets which literally scoop up the fish, transferring them back into a long and narrow "cod-head," the final residence of the fish before they are brought aboard. Besides groundfish, a few species of flatfish, mostly flounder, are also caught by this method (something to ponder when next you enjoy lemon sole or crab-stuffed flounder fillets at your favorite restaurant.)

## Gillnetters

Gillnetting usually takes place out of smaller craft and is altogether a different technology from dragging. A series of plastic monofilament nets are strung together so as to create a virtual wall of death for fish. The bottom of the netwall is weighted by lead-filled line. The top line, on the other hand, has floats at intervals all along its length, giving enough buoyancy to hold the net upright as a wall, but not enough to float the net back up to the surface. At fishing depths, this net is invisible to the fish, which find on entering a mesh or window of the net that its head may enter but not its

**Cod** — one of the first ground-fish caught within sight of the fishing stations, pickled in brine and called "cor-fish".

**Opposite** A medium-sized dragger rests on her laurels, and her crew's Sunday dinner, in a small harbor near Schoodic

Manana Island **above left** overlooks, and helps to make up, Monhegan's tenuous harbor. It has been a mark to fishermen for nearly 400 years.

Small, high, and off-shore, Monhegan's relative advantages always overcame its small and not especially protected harbor **above right**. It has been a fishing station, then plantation, since the reign of the first Elizabeth.

body. In their attempts to back out of the meshes, the net engages their gills, thus trapping and asphixiating the fish. The past decade has seen an ever larger portion of Maine's groundfish thus caught, raising considerable controversy over product quality and the disposition of unretrieved lost gear, which can go on fishing forever, unless finally snarled and balled-up by entangled sharks or large sea mammals. Divers tell us that several of the more notable shipwrecks in the gulf of Maine are literally encapsulated in "hungdown" fishing gear, some of it still fishing.

Here and there along the coast a few fishermen regularly go out after swordfish and tuna, using harpoons; but this is generally "headboat" trade, hired-out boats and gear to sportsfishermen. Similarly, rod and reel fishing is not especially prominent to this coast; though considerable striped bass and bluefish are taken in season at places like Popham Beach and other sandy shores. The return of the Atlantic Salmon to the Penobscot River (after nearly a century!) have sportsmen ready with high waterproof boots and beer coolers in enthusiastic numbers.

The other great fishery of the coast is for herring, which possesses two technologies inherent to their catch: purse seining, and so-called "stop-fishing," the latter method disappearing in recent years, as did weir-fishing (cove trap-fishing). Herring are the *sine qua non* of schooling fish, and each year enormous schools of them appear from the westward, offshore, where the night-riding purse seiners

await them. The fishermen literally surround vast numbers of the silvery fish with a wall of tightly meshed net, which is then "pursed." When the bottom is closed, great powerblocks gather in the net, bundling the fish until finally sardine carriers can come alongside the purse and pump the fish aboard. These fish then go either to packing plants and various fish markets or become bait fish for Maine's incomparable lobstering industry.

Vessels engaged in the sardine (herring) trade tie up to the McLoon wharf in Rockland **below**. Tending weir, stop- and purse-seining operations, these boats serve many markets, including fish used for bait, food additives, cattle feed and fertilizer, as well as canned sardines, herring steaks and fillets and kippers.

**Overleaf** Clam diggers in Cushing wade through the flooding tide, returning after several hours bent to "fork and hod."

This empty seine dory **right**, moored in a small island cove, is really a sign saying "this cove is mine!", meaning that its owner claims the right to "stop-fish" any schools of herring that enter the cove.

There are other fin fisheries along the coast: alewives taken from river estuaries in the early spring; smelts; an occasional load of pogie (menhaden), or mackerel sold here and there, but these are all considered minor efforts and markets. All things considered, Maine must these days be regarded as a transitional fin-fishing state; somewhere between traditional practices and capitalization and those of the future, which no doubt will exploit not only the currently marketable species with greater vigor and efficiency but also bring to the American table many heretofore undiscovered marine treats.

## Lobsters and Lobstering

Lobstering is the essence of the Maine fisheries. There are greater tonnages of other species and more money from them, but it is in lobstering that Maine finds its primary maritime identity. The species is fished out of nearly every harbor, from end to end of the coast, by roughly ten thousand fishermen, including sternmen—the crew who assist the skipper-owner lobstermen. With annual landings averaging 20 million pounds and worth about 40 million dollars, this is a lot of bread and butter earned for a lot of family tables! That is the genius of the business. It is spread-

out, and access to it is relatively easy for those who qualify by residence, fishing-gang acceptance, and competence. A typical fishing family child will have his own small outboard and "string of gear" as early as nine years of age and often will be making as much money at it in early teenage years as his teachers make at the local school. It is a compellingly *macho* enterprise!

Whether you are looking out over a small bight, cove, or harbor at a handful of lobster-boats or at one of the really large, concentrated fleets, you gaze upon much more than merely a collection of marine craft. It is symbolic of an entire lifestyle—a culture of extraordinary character and integrity in this day and age of increasing homogeneity in society. To be sure, many changes have been introduced into the trade since the not-long-ago times of 20 cent (or less) lobsters packed in seaweed and barrels, but, still, the expectations and values of the lobsterman largely remain those of his ancestors. Working independently on the water in a small, self-owned craft and catching a wild marine animal for a free market—lobstering can be considered an anachronistic enterprise, a business that allows for individuality in sharp contrast with the massive organization of institutional networks that our civilization has become! Not surprisingly, the society that lobstering supports tends to be a tight one: traditional, privy, competitive, and belligerent on one hand, yet cooperative and very canny, on the other hand. To succeed season after season, a lobsterman must be extraordinarily able. He must know the ways of the sea—weather,

A classic scene of the lobster
fishery: boats, wharf, fish-house and pier, here
standing by at Beals Island,
a place long famous for its many builders of
high-quality lobsterboats of
distinct type.

Off Stonington, a man in a punt **above** tends moored crates of lobsters. In summertime, many fishermen will hold some of their lobsters for private customers and special occasions.

tides, waves; the ways of lobsters—their behavior and bottom; the ways of boats—their possibilities, limitations, and maintenance, and certainly of the sheer fragility and cyclical nature of life. Visitors to the Maine coast often wonder aloud at how reticent local fishermen are in their conversation, and how often a sort of ironic humor permeates what they say, even in answer to a simple question. The reason is that, quite simply, no experienced fisherman really believes in answers, and feels strongly that those who seek out information that is hard, fast, and straightforward are plainly being foolish. The attitudes and values most people learn from their professions are often applied to the rest of their lives, to some degree or other, and small-craft, inshore fishermen are no exception, for very good reason. If they have learned to be taciturn and skeptical, it is because the future is unpredictable and not always within one's control— especially in these fishing towns, where their livelihood is subject to the fluctuations of both nature and the economy.

There is also a good deal more sophistication to the lobster business than meets the naive outsider's eye. New lobsterboats are not cheap. Thirty-five thousand dollars for a new one these days is not unusual. And a good string of gear—500 traps with warps, toggles, and bouys—will run between 15 and 20 thousand dollars. Add radios, depth sounders, Loran, and their maintenance, and you get another 10 thousand dollars. A day's hauling may use 100 gallons of fuel and 20 bushels of bait (at about nine dollars per bushel). A little sharp penciling here will raise the eyebrows of even the most urbane accountant! Of course, the wear and tear of the marine environment is awesome, and loss of gear is common and continual. Consider the fact that the engine of a lobsterboat, moving at normal cruising speed, puts out the power that the same (automotive) engine block would have to produce to move a large American family sedan at over 100 miles per hour! Gaze out on that harbor, and wonder at it!

Ashore, the round of life gravitates about the wharves, fishhouses, and kitchens. There is gossip—weather portents, catches, and prices. The fishermen must always be calculating, guessing and second-guessing the movement of the lobsters and their fellow fishermen. Lobsterpots must be continually

patched and repaired, warps shortened or lengthened, new stuff gone over, painted, or otherwise prepared for their service. Community life in these places is generally rich, almost feverish, during holiday season. Traditional American cooking is alive and well in these parts, and oceangoing appetites are neither hesitant nor demure. Local stores cannot keep enough canning jars in stock; wine and cider jugs down in cellars have loose tops.

Lobsterman Richard Williams, of Vinalhaven **left**, heads-up a pot in the old Dyer family fish-house.

The tombstone of Captain Smalley,
standing in a tranquil churchyard, is a
commonplace reminder that
the lives of Maine's seafarers were daily at the
mercy of the deep.

## The Life of a Lobster

The lobsters themselves are most remarkable creatures. A crustacean, Homaris Americanus is extraordinarily ubiquitious, long-lived, and mobile over the continental shelf of the Northeast. While they are caught commercially from Cape May eastward, gourmets of the toothsome animal rightly claim that a cold-water lobster (real *Maine*) has a sweeter and more delicate flavor compared to his war-water cousins, making "Maine lobster" the usual designation in restaurants and markets nationwide, no matter what the actual source. It is ironic that older Maine citizens can vividly remember catching lobsters out of *tidepools* (!) and taking them home to the family table because they could not afford fancier fare, like milk and bacon. Even today, summer visitors are shocked at the blasé attitude taken toward lobsters in Maine fishing towns. Back home, dining out means that best clothes are donned and credit cards tentatively extracted; in Maine, the most delectable lobster is wolfed-down with mundane and unceremonious relish!

Like many other marine creatures, the life cycle of the lobster is not very well understood and is, in any case, extremely hazardous. Having an outside skeleton or shell (exoskeleton), lobsters must molt (regularly shed their shells) in order to grow. Being carnivors during their hard-shell periods, eating mostly other crustaceans and carrion, these animals are rendered virtually helpless during their molting. This condition is exacerbated by the fact that adult lobsters can breed only during times when the female is without her shell. The female either digs a hole in the bottom mud or finds a rock interstice in which to hide for the molting process. Then she exudes a powerful biochemical signal that attracts males, who gather round the hole to await a chance to mate and also to protect the lady from predators. After all, nearly every creeping, crawling, and swimming thing in the ocean would love to eat a defenseless lobster.

Once successfully fertilized and graced by a new and larger shell, the female can safely emerge and go about the business of recouping her strength and growing eggs, which grow in "berried" clusters under her tail. These in term hatch, the spawn becoming part of the sea's enormous stock of zooplankton for several water-born molts. There is a hole, then, in our scientific understanding; but it is now thought that these millions of planktonic lobsters seek out certain benthic currents, which distribute them throughout their territory. They continue to molt in rapid succession while this goes on, and eventually they become heavy enough to lose their bouyancy and drop down through the water column to the bottom. Here, four to five years must pass, and many more molts, before they become sexually mature and can continue their ancient life cycle. All the while, a stupendous toll is taken on the lobster supply by physical as well as biological processes.

We do not know how old a lobster can become. Several 40-pound specimens are known, but many reputable fishermen, especially old timers, scoff at the size of these, comparing the claw sizes with the occasional truly giant claws that come up in set fishing gear. There may be, down there somewhere, a 100-pound lobster! Maine fishermen will never tell us, for the state of Maine has stringent size limitations on the lobsters that can be sold, even possessed, by its fishermen. It is a conservation measure, the theory being that all lobsters must be allowed to grow to sexual maturity at least, and then kept free to breed in significant fecundity, should they luck through the fishery and get over a certain size, roughly around five pounds under current law.

## Catching Lobsters

In spite of all the fancy gear and modern science, each area and harbor has its own variation of equipment and technique, indeed art, in catching lobsters. From afar, and to the untrained eye, lobsterboats all look more or less alike. To fishermen, however, no two boats are anything alike, showing enormous

**Overleaf** As they steam home, gillnetters clean their catch, to the very intense interest of thousands of seagulls in outer Penobscot Bay.

The **starfish**, also called a sea star, lives in tidepools and preys on bivalves like clam and oyster, prying open their shells with its powerful tentacles.

variation in hull form, layout, rig, and gear. Any aspiring fisherman's youngster can tell you that this one is a Noviboat (named after Nova Scotia, where this broad, hefty type of boat is built), that one a Jonesport Boat, a Bruno, a Holland, an Eaton, a Holstrom, a Dyer, and a Chandler. On it goes, different boat types tending to be favored locally on account of their special features appropriate to local waters and conditions. Furthermore, even though every lobsterman places a number-brand on his fishing gear, such identification is hardly necessary among the local men, for each fisherman rigs his gear differently from everyone else. The size, shape, heading, and warping methods employed in the pots (traps) give a man's gear distinct individual-ity.

Roughly three-quarters of the Maine lobstermen fish their gear about seven months of the year, hauling their boats and gear ashore for the dead of winter. The remaining quarter fish year-round, having to "lengthen-out" their warps so as to fish the deeper water offshore, sometimes as far as 40 miles offshore in depths to 70 fathoms. As we mentioned, lobsters are very mobile, and when the warm weather "shedding season," the inshore breeding season, is over, most of the lobsters move offshore into deeper water. This, of course, creates a more hazardous, thinner, yet expensive fishery, but the price is commensurately greater, so the game remains worthwhile for those fishermen with the equipment and heart to play it. Winter lobster-men are true *seamen* in the old-fashioned meaning of the term!

Lobster is a marvelous food. It is won at considerable labor, risk, and cost, but it is an effort the fishermen of the coast of Maine are pleased to assume.

## The Secondary Fisheries

Maine in general, and certainly her coast in particular, has from the beginning been con-sidered a source of raw skills and products rather than a place for sophisticated value-adding, marketing, and distribution. To this day, Mainers resist the idea of social infra-structure, with its image of paper-pushing, forms to fill out, specialized experts on this and that, and people in uniform business clothes running around going to meetings. These feelings run deep in the Maine grain and attract people from elsewhere of like senti-ment. Few coastal industries point out these native sensibilities better than the state's secondary marine fisheries. Perhaps the only exception is the coast's plethora of artists, artisans, and jobbers, which we will discuss elsewhere in the book.

## Clams

In less well-to-do households along the coast, when the winter comes and cash is scarce, a man will often be heard to say, "I got feet and a clamfork!" This statement of mixed deter-mination and pride, of course, belies the regu-

lar efforts of hundreds of people who earn their full-time professional living as clam and worm diggers. For generations, digging the muddy bivalves has been a reliable means of earning money to place food on otherwise hard-pressed tables. Clams have also been a tasty source of food in lean times. The soft-shelled clam, ubiquitous in Maine's tidal flats, offers splendid eating and enjoys nationwide markets in effective competition with the harder and more robust-tasting clams from other areas. While every township has its number of full- and part-time clammers, which is generally a function of what the local supply and market will bare, the most famous center for the industry is Waldoboro. A highly competent "mosquito fleet" daily goes forth in high-speed outboards to exploit the flats in all directions; traveling 40 miles from home base is not thought to be excessive for the dozen-odd bushels a day the best diggers are capable of digging.

Of course, all natives and summer folk alike try to make a Maine clambake an annual event, under whatever auspices can qualify as an excuse—national holiday, birthday, anniversary—whatever works. Some misbehavior is expected and forgiven at these celebrations, and no one pays the slightest attention to his diet.

A typical clambake begins with a very large driftwood fire built in some depression on the beach. When the coals are mighty and deep, a surfeit of seaweed is applied over the coals. Then a layer of potatoes (wrapped in foil) is applied, and a bit more seaweed. Next comes a like layer of corn, followed by a layer (a big pile actually) of lobsters and crabs, and finally a big layer of clams and (in recent years) mussels. This whole mess is then doubly covered in more rockweed, and the entire enterprise covered by a tarpaulin.

While this smokes and steams away, the adults gossip and tell lies and the kids try to kill themselves in feats of foolishness and bravado. After 45 minutes or so, the whole pile is dismantled, distributed according to rank and gluttony, and consumed. The party ends when (1) the kids become impossible (2) the libations-of-choice run out (3) the tide comes in, eliminating the beach. If you've never experienced a Maine clambake, life has

The **blue crab** of the Atlantic coast is marketed for food as a soft-shelled crab after it has molted but before its new shell has hardened.

passed you by! (There is also a natives-only autumn version of this, involving sea-duck breasts and pork ribs.)

Anyway, clamming is an important secondary Maine coast fishery. These days, it is much plagued by problems of pollution off of economically developing watersheds. Clam flats, after all, are only half-land, half-the-time!

## Worms

Then there is the worm industry. The center of the activity and trade is at Wiscasset. Why worms, you might ask. Ask any sports fisherman. These foot-long, segmented creatures seem to have magic in their bodies—ask any fish in North America; there isn't a fish that does not have a craving for them! Fewer than a hundred people in Maine make their living from the worm industry, but thousands of sport fishermen benefit enormously from their enterprise.

## Scallops

Scalloping is altogether a more important fishery but still remains a secondary fishing activity when compared with the principals. Like shrimp, they are a seasonal, winter catch, both by general availability and the law. Most scallopers go lobstering in summer. But what a treat the scallop is—and valuable! An entire winter's day of dragging heavy, metal-meshed gear over the relatively small areas where these swimming bivalves are known to "bed-up" may produce a single pailful of scallop meats, but at six to seven dollars a pound, that single pail will bring home the bacon for the skipper and crew, who would otherwise, and not so profitably, have to seek employment ashore.

The rest of America has only recently discovered what Europeans and Mainers have known for generations—that the blue mussel

is deliciously good food. The number of wild, naturally occurring mussels caught has gone up rapidly in recent years, and the artificial raising of mussels for commercial market is annually doubling in volume sales, as lounge-dwellers and restaurant owners discover that these pearly mollusks are every bit as desirable as the more traditional oyster or cherry-stone clam of appetizer fame.

## Crabs

The same can be said of Maine crabs. Until the late 1970s, Maine's fishermen considered the three most common species of inshore crabs to be veritable pests, worthless bait-stealers. Of course, local people had always cleaned out the occasional pailful for home consumption, and summer visitors often looked forward to the small local grocery stores and lunch counters along the coast, where the local crab meat and rolls were common summer fare for years. But, against the more famous "blues" of the Chesapeake Bay, and the dungeness, snows and kings of the West Coast, Maine's reds, rocks, whitelegs and pickytoes were virtual unknowns in the national marketplace. This is slowly but surely, and justifiably, changing as marketing people discover the hitherto unknown virtues of the Northeast's crab offerings. As people discover the relatively lighter, sweeter flavor

Seiner and windjammer **center** share mooring space at Bar Harbor; a sister windjammer is "making-out-by" in the distance.

A lobsterman, his trade, and his shop. For every hour spent at sea, setting and hauling gear, there are at least as many spent ashore in trapshops and fish-houses manufacturing the equipment. This requires as much patience and skill as the fishing itself **left**.

of the Maine product, in everything from cocktail claws to sandwich spreads, more and more fishermen will value and bring to market what not long ago was a despised product.

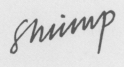

Maine's shrimp, of course, never suffered from such prejudice. The problem with shrimp has been one of very unpredictable supply from year to year. These rather small, sweet shrimp have a quality all their own; they are often treated and eaten as if they were candy by coastal Mainers. Shrimp may legally be taken by small drags, within sight of the shore, all along the coast. For their qualities of sweetness they are rivaled, perhaps, only by the small shrimps of the Pacific Northwest, which are thought to be as good, but in no way finer!

Three other fisheries deserve mention, not for their current volume, but rather for their future promise. United States consumers are becoming much better informed about diet,

and we seem to be developing our palates towards a greater tolerance for variety in foods. Thirty years ago we were a nation locked into the idea that fish were, or should be, either white or pink, and fried in any case. Those days are gone, happily. Seafood looks better and better all the time, not just for its health-giving qualities, but for the enormous *variety* it offers. In Maine the telltale signs are appearing in new markets opening up for eels, once thought loathsome; for squid, once considered just an odd but effective bait for other creatures, and even sea urchins, whose roe begins to grace the occasional cracker. (Here we are taking our cues from the Japanese, who have enjoyed roe for 1,000 years!)

Bycatches, such as monkfish, sea catfish, and wolffish are finding their tails in fancy New York, Philadelphia, and Baltimore restaurants; and newly discovered beds of mahogany quohogs wait their turn in the future of Maine's fisheries. Even the ubiquitous periwinkle and whelks are getting dipped into experimentally prepared homemade sauces and being discovered.

The coast of Maine is an enormous resource place, and its variety of seafood is only one of the assets that give the region its unique character.

**Mussels** — enjoyed by Mainers and Europeans for generations, but only recently appreciated by the rest of America.

# PENOBSCOT BAY

Thirty miles out to sea sits lonely Matinicus Rock. Since its lighthouse was automated a few years ago, only the endangered puffins and razor-billed auks are there to be the gatekeepers of mighty Penobscot, Maine's most expansive and diverse bay. The mainland seems to want to cradle it at the location between Port Clyde and up through the western shores of Rockport-Camden, Lincoln-Belfast, and Castine to Sedgewick, but then it loses its concentration and begins to fragment at easterly Deer Isle. The Penobscot explodes into a multitude of islands in Merchants Row, giving the last of the work to beautifully wild Isle au Haut. Swirling about its inner reaches, the Fox Islands want to dominate, and just miss doing so in the lights of Islesboro, Eagle and Butter Islands and their companions in the northern bay. In the old parlance, "'Tis a fair piece o' briny!"

The brilliant blue, yellow and vermilion bill of the **puffin**, capable of carrying several fish at a time, gives the bird its nickname of "sea parrot."

## Rockland

Moment to moment, Owls Head Light winks at her younger brother light, located at the end of Rockland's mile-long breakwater, only a few thousand yards away across the harbor mouth. Originally part of Thomaston and called Shore Village, Rockland became her present self in 1848, when the city's vast limestone deposits gave its citizens the identity and economic clout to sue for separation. Only a few fragments of the town's old limeworks remain, and in any case are not featured by the chamber of commerce. Indeed, even the modern limeworks facility (officially in Thomaston but whose heart is in Rockland) is

Rockport Lighthouse **right** guards a poor harbor with many fine yachts and boats. André the Seal, a once-orphaned pup who has adopted Rockport as home and annually commutes by sea and fin from the New England Aquarium in Boston, gives this harbor odd distinction.

**Opposite** A refurbished structure with some eye-catching features along the roadside can mean only one thing — one of the coast's many hundreds of antique barns. This one is in Wiscasset.

in what is presumed to be temporary doldrums after three ownerships in recent times. (The last ownership was to an American Indian entrepreneurial commission in the use of hard-fought-for law-suit awards stemming from white land appropriations in central Maine in the nineteenth century.) In any case, Rockland is a working town in the best sense of it. Cleaned up, developing a renewed sense of pride, Rockland is a city full of skilled and hard-working people, who generally work in small shops. Well known for its Lobster Festival and astoundingly successful Marine Colloids Company (which converts seaweed emulsives into hundreds of modern products), the city's heart and core is perhaps best reflected in the Bicknell Company, one of the few remaining manufacturers of specialist quarrying, smithing, and stoneworking tools in the nation. Here steel ships are repaired, traditional sailing schooners are built, and high-tech yachts conceived. But overall, the town's strength resides in the exchange of an individual's skilled service for cash. It may be the best town in America for, say, inventors and entrepreneurs. Somewhere, someone in Rockland can make just what you want, very inexpensively, and on time. This is some of the "old Maine" in new dress, offering the boutiques and fine cuisine as well, but not being hung-up on them ...

## Rockport and Camden

Meanwhile, down the shore, we find Rockport and Camden, who march to a different drummer. While the average tourist will find many of Maine's coastal towns very pleasant and attractive, worthy of architectural dotage and exploration, there is something about Camden-Rockport that has these same visitors calling realtors and brokers back home! With just enough "Maine-type stuff" to keep them quaint, enough industrial effort to keep them honest, and all the lifestyle facilities for which one could reasonably ask in rural America, Camden-Rockport is the only island of communal fabric.

Rockland **center** is one of the Maine Coast's several reawakening commercial towns. Her large and well-located harbor combines with a good work ethic among its citizens to promise a bright future.

The isolation and starkness of Matinicus Rock **left** makes it both an important puffin rookery and a valued lighthouse location.

East of Brunswick could be called a new-age, information-economy community. It is a major center for publishing. This is the home of the Maine Coast Artists Association, one of the most prestigious of such organizations in the Northeast; the same could be said of Rockport's Maine Photographic Workshop. Maine's largest fleet of working windjammers (sailing holiday vessels) are here, and the yachting facilities are the best, though crowded, as are the eateries and shops. Mount Battie, one of the nearby gorgeous Camden Hills, is accessible by car. Rockport is the archetypal "nice town." Bring your wallet.

## Art, Artists, and Artisans

Shortly after the Civil War (for which there is a many-named monument in every village and town along the coast) Maine shores have been host to a continual stream of creative artists, some of the best our civilization has ever offered among them. Amidst artists themselves, certain places immediately come to mind as artist's communities—Kennebunk, Portland, Brunswick-Harpswells, Wiscasset–Boothbay, Cushing, Rockport-Camden, Monhegan Island, Bar Harbor, and Northeast Harbor. But these places are simply centers, hubs around which inspired and skilled work converges from village and countryside all along the coast. Every few miles has its painters and writers, sculptors and poets; these are some solidly commited year-rounders who are reinforced each summer by

95

Part of Camden's windjammer fleet **right** lies ready for another week of summer sailing fun. Many of these vessels are refurbished ships from the great age of commercial sail.

droves of artists from metropolitan and academic centers all over the country.

The coastal villages have many small summer galleries, and many a church, school auditorium, and town hall will regularly resound to musical performances of all sorts. Small repertory theatrical companies dot the coastal map, and many communities have enthusiastic amateur musical and dramatic productions as a regular feature of their calendar.

There are other areas of New England where artists tend to gather—the Berkshires, Central Vermont, Cape Cod and so on, but none is so extensive or so reliably prolific as the coast of Maine. To be sure, these shores attract millions who simply want to relax and enjoy the sea and shore and the special qualities of the shore's look and feel; but among them are many who come specifically to renew their spirit through the arts that thrive here.

Historical reasons are partly responsible for the amount and quality of these arts. When the aristocracies of the Atlantic Seaboard cities began to "discover" the coast of Maine and to establish cottage and "rustication" communities, they naturally brought with them not only their liking for, and participation in, the arts, they also attracted those who would court their favor and patronage. These shores are also so beautiful in their own right that it would be a poor and insensitive artist who would not be inspired from what the area offers to an artistic sensibility and talent. It is not only beautiful, though, it is also challenging, for the coastal light is special, the weather extraordinarily diverse, and the confluences of water and land so changing that the area is a study in intense variation! Furthermore, people of the coast have a native integrity, a tolerance of and appreciation for individual character that artists of all persuasions find attractive. Indeed, it is not simply a matter of appreciation. There is also *participation*, for the native coastal Mainer tends to be very dexterous and multiskilled himself. He often recognizes similar artistic leanings in others who show skill and talent, even though the art form may not be his own bailiwick. Even at that, talented native artists, *per se*, are abundant: the fisherman's wife and her watercolors, the boatbuilder's beautiful furniture, the auto mechanic and his metal sculptures,

the postmistress and her macramé, the quilters, weavers, potters, caners, photographers, musicians, and so forth. Creativity and the coast of Maine just seem to go together.

*Reaching the Sea*

Heading down the shore by automobile, Maine's coastal Route One finally begins to allow glimpses of the sea, here of western Penobscot Bay. So indented is the usual coast morphology that it is only by feeder arteries that the land traveler gets a look at salt water, the exceptions being where estuaries make up inland far enough for the Route One bridges to afford a glance. But between Camden and Bucksport the sea is regularly in view, and except in fog always offers a fine sight.

This brings up a general problem on the Maine coast, especially this area, the "midcoast Region"— namely, that there is very little public access to the water. While all shore towns have public landings, this region has very few public beaches or waterside access of any sort. Indeed, between Owls Head, which has a small state park, and Bucksport, more than an hour's drive between the two, there is only one access place that could be called a beach, a small one at Duck Trap, in Lincolnville, just beyond Camden. Beach access is becoming a very large problem nationwide, as ownership and its nine-tenths of the law recognizes the dollar value of the

# I S L A N D   S H E E P

Considerable logistics were required
when the owners of Allen Island decided to
reintroduce sheep to the traditional
island economy along the coast of Maine. Land
was cleared, pasturage reestablished,
the sheep acquired; then loaded, transported,
and finally timidly introduced
to their new home. For the first few months, the
sheep spent a good deal of time
hiding under weather-stressed trees and
woods, looking about their new
envionment. Today, they constitute a healthy
and enthusiastic flock, and a
model for other island owners to emulate.

Once an industrial and fishing town, Camden **right** today is almost frantically active in recreation and tourism. Says one Camdenite, "Our bright future is happening now!"

land's edges over the public weal. Maine, for all of its Yankee if pugnacious tolerance, is no exception.

## Coastal Towns

Anyway, here, at least, we often get to look at the ocean by car. The boatman, of course, has the best of it all along. Substantial hills are also in sight from here eastward, each prominent in its own right. Blue Hill, which we will meet soon, and Cadillac Mountain, on Mount Desert of the next chapter, are only the most well-known out of a regional mountain community of over a hundred, each distinct and subject to much local affection.

Out of Camden and through this more eclectic countryside, the first port of call is Lincolnville Beach, a stop interesting not so much for its beach, *per se*, as for the terminal for the Islesboro Ferry. This boat serves Islesboro's year-round, commuter and summer season populus, whose homes and harbors are the picture of gracious elegance. The relatively flat terrain of the island, its generally along-shore roadways and attentive ferry schedule makes Islesboro an ideal day-trip for bicyclists.

Just beyond Lincolnville Beach comes Duck Trap, named for its ancient preference among duckdom as a molting place, and so consequently also an old Indian and settlers' center for massive cooperative game harvests. Every year, mature ducks follow up the fledging season with a period of relative inactivity while they shed old, wornout feathers for a fresh new set. They feed heavily during this period, building up fat, all for the long autumn migratory flight that follows (except for eiderducks, many of whom stay in the region all winter). They are flightless and nearly helpless during this period, and their tendency to congregate makes them easy pickings, illegal pickings in modern times, but the ancient activity lives on in the place name.

The shoreline from Duck Trap to Belfast is very bold and "steep-to," relieved only by the small bights of Little Harbor, Saturday Cove (made famous by 20 years of articles in the monthly *National Fisherman* by Captain Perc Sane, alias Mike Brown, of Saturday Cove), and Little River. The prevailing township here is Northport, and its dominant footnote is

Decrepit remains of nineteenth-century lime kilns **above** languish in autumn sunlight near Rockport. In their heyday, these furnaces would burn 1,700 cords of wood a week.

Belted Galloway beef cattle **below** make a stunning and unusual sight on a byway through Rockport's affluent countryside.

The three-masted schooner
*Victory Chimes* at her usual berth in
Rockland. She is one of the best-kept
and navigated vessels on the coast.

probably the Temple Heights Community, a summer religious colony and the only shore-side one of its type or kind east of Oak Bluffs, on Martha's Vineyard in Massachusetts. Here matters of the spirit are celebrated in an environment of deep family feeling and close clusters of compellingly quaint gingerbread cottages.

Belfast is another coastal town finding renewed vigor out of its industrial past. Originally another shipbuilding center, Belfast suffered several decades of being more or less mono-industrial, the most recent being chick-

ens, with 150,000 broilers being processed daily. Such monolithic economic activity is now defunct, as the city finds its once languishing neighborhoods being rapidly refurbished by young professional people with eyes and investments focused on the future. The downtown area's marvelous Edwardian architecture deserves the renewed appreciation that is clearly in store for it; an abiding local wish being that the sound folk culture of the city is not traded off as gentrification accompanies that appreciation. It is precisely a Mainer's town, and it is hoped that it remains so.

Across the river, in Searport township, we come to Moose Point Park, an ideal traveler's stopping place with extraordinary views of the bay, and a good place to air the car, walk the dog, picnic, and try once again to convince the kids that Acadia Park is just an hour away, should that be the family quest. It will not be our quest, though, for after a bit more of these western bay shores, we will turn northabout onto the Blue Hill Peninsula, and so to the eastern Penobscot Bay region. Meanwhile,

The Isleboro Light and Maine State Ferry slip **above** sits in readiness for a major overhaul in preparation for the island's newer, larger ferry boat. Most of the inhabited islands of the coast find themselves pressed to provide adequate social services, including transportation.

Camden's snug, and crowded, harbor nestles on the mainland shore of Penobscot Bay **below**. From the top of Mount Battie, ancient Matinicus Island looms on the far horizon.

**Overleaf** The old and kept-as-it-is Olson House in Cushing will be familiar to Andrew Wyeth buffs as the scene of his famous painting, *Christina's World*. **101**

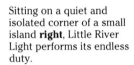

Sitting on a quiet and isolated corner of a small island **right**, Little River Light performs its endless duty.

Searsport Harbor, for all its lack of aesthetic qualities, is the second largest and most important deepwater port on the coast, after Portland. This is a terminus for the Bangor and Aroostook Railroad, here discharging potatoes and paper onto ship and receiving in kind oil, coal, grains, and of all things, huge cargoes of raw tapioca, used to coat Maine's primary industrial product—*paper*. The town itself is looking rather bare these days since its stately elms succombed to the Dutch Elm blight, but its fine sea captains' homes remain as testament to the era of "sea-widows" and their large families. The local Penobscot Marine Museum has a fine collection of ship's logs from those times, and it does for the human dimension of the age of sail what the Maritime Museum in Bath does for the records of ship construction. The paintings, models, and dioramas of these places are excellent, to be sure, but their real strengths lie in their splendid archives. Neither are to be missed by the marine buff. They are the true stuff of sea-going adventure!

Nearby Sears Island, wooded and uninhabited, has had enormous piles of bureaucratic red tape and litigious concern heaped upon it as the last decade and a half would have embellished it with, in turn, being a site for nuclear power, an oil delivery terminal, and finally a coal-fired electrical generation facility. The last of these matters has by no means yet been heard ...

The next township, Stockton Springs, is

easily missed via the highway. There are some perfectly extraordinary dwelling structures along the road, but the temptation to bypass the turn into town and onto Cape Jellison is well worth smothering, for here we find the mouth of the illimitable Penobscot Rivers, overseen by Fort Pownell. This was first established by the British in 1759 against the French and was twice burned by the English garrison to keep it out of enemy (American) hands during the Revolution. Today the structure is a museum, housing among other things Indian artifacts excavated from the site in recent times.

It is the river itself, though, that has such physical presence and historical power and which compels our interest. For here is the ancient traditional gateway to the vast northern interior reaches of the state, whose waters are the silent guardians of the legends, the blood, sweat, and tears of generations of woodsmen, lumbermen, draymen, and most particularly the rivermen who brought to market a billion feet of logs down this waterway. Bangor, at the tidal head of the river, is of course the *sine qua non* old lumbertown—today a city like all others in contemporary pursuits but proud of its past (its bar-room brawling and ladies of the night notwithstanding.) The Paul Bunyan legend began here, and genteel society first learned of the glories of this watershed from Henry David Thearman, who personally chased down the places of Norumbega, the "city of gold" which first

An elegant, if poignant, widow's
walk graces one of Belfast's many old
captain's homes.

The first church built in Belfast
is the pride and joy of its Congregational
flock. The church has been serving
its community since the 1790s.

The Atlantic **salmon** has returned to the Penobscot River after a break of over a century.

dazzled mariners to seek out fortune and the Northwest Passage in these and other Acadian waters.

The Atlantic salmon is only recently returned to the river after more than a century of tannin and particulate pollution from the great river drives that built houses from here to China and beyond. It is worthwhile to note that veritable shelves of books have been written about this river and its past, just as for many of the other regions we have mentioned so briefly in this coastal survey.

We cross the river ourselves at the next town of Prospect, named for its uniquely high and—well, prospective municipal survey of the river. Below it is Fort Knox (no, not *that* Fort Knox!) which guards the last episode of the river, where it splits to make Verona Island Township before emptying into the bay, just across from Bucksport, into which we pass after the picturesque Waldo-Hancock Bridge is negotiated. A milltown from its inception in the mid-eighteenth century, Bucksport remains one today, and the traveling family has the unusual opportunity here to visit an operating paper mill—the St. Regis Paper Company here is open to visitors by appointment.

For good or ill, Bucksport, and certainly its neighboring town of Verona, are easily passed by the traveler. They come into view, flash by, and are left behind. The true glories of a place are not seen on the run, and of course the secrets of a place take more time and effort than the glories. Fascinating houses? Revealing cemeteries? Lovely little parks and byways? All Maine coastal towns have them, waiting to be discovered by those not in a hurry.

We hurry on nevertheless! The Blue Hill Peninsula awaits our stewardship. Because it is a peninsula, we find here a pattern of Maine settlement that is very common but which, because of our coastal press to get downeast, we have not been prone to notice. This is the variegated, almost mosaic character of the human habitation pattern. Very substantial blocks of land in wilderness are demarcated by old roadways along which people live, rather lined up and down the roads, albeit at varying set-back locations. This was the common pattern of development for most of America, for obvious reasons, but time and economy have generally subdivided the old

Nearly full, the moon shines down through the slim towers of the Waldo-Hancock Bridge **center**, one of the most perfectly proportioned of its type anywhere.

Could there be a more American picture of an American town? The genius of native community design is shown off by Bucksport **above**, across the Penobscot River from Fort Knox (no, not *that* Fort Knox!).

Low tides allow the coastal photographer access to the lower reaches of the intertidal zone, and so a dramatic slant back over the rocks, up into Stonington village **below**.

There is much adventure to
be found along cliffs. These, at Acadia
National Park on Mount Desert
Island, give stony testimony to the sea's
awesome power. Winter storm
waves will wash right over the top of them!

Homes and shops of Stonington **left** huddle along the bluff that transects the village and gives presence to its busy waterfront.

blocks of land. Not so in this countryside, where a person can walk out his back door and move in a straight line for at least a couple of miles before encountering someone else's backyard. (The township of Penobscot is a textbook lesson in this phenomenon.) Here the inhabitants are engaged in retirement's pursuits: blueberry canning, some peat mining, and much enjoyment of the contiguous blocks of wild land.

## Historic Castine

But soon comes Castine, and another discussion entirely. The very name rings in the American ear. Originally founded by the Massachusetts Plymouth Colony in 1626 as a trading station, between then and the War of 1812 this vital port was wrenched by violence back and forth among English, American, French, and Dutch forces fully *nine times*! Here in this peaceful town, the attentive traveler will find more than 100 historical markers describing or commemorating two centuries of carnage and confrontation—surely the most pathetic one being the American Penobscot Expedition of 1779. This was the major English naval base east of New York, and from here originated a major portion of English naval harassment of New England. The Penobscot Bay islanders were especially hard-pressed on account of the British regular practice of stripping out all of the island farms for provisions. It *had* to stop, and so 40 ships were dispatched to Castine to take the Harbor's Fort George. Over 500 Americans lost their lives in the unsuccessful attempt. Only two of the American ships

**Overleaf** Lowering clouds cast a mellow gray light on a stretch of the Maine coast seen from Hurricane Island. **111**

escaped, the others being captured, sunk, or burned and scuttled to prevent their capture. One of these has been discovered and archaeologically explored off the shores of Northport. Former hero Paul Revere was one of the several officers permanantly discredited by the catastrophe. The Fort George facility, nearby Fort Madison, and the Wilson Museum in Castine are all display institutions, open to the public and dedicated to the memorial of this and the rest of Castine's extraordinary past.

Maine Maritime Academy is also located in Castine. The second largest merchant training school in the country, it is generally considered to be the best of them all—high praise in a world ever more dependent not just on shipping but also on competent quality shipping. Its training vessel, State of Maine, is open to the public when in port.

## Deer Isle

Whether by land or sea, the visitor cannot disregard Deer Isle in good faith. By land from Castine, we pass through the especially beautiful fishing and boatbuilding town of Brookville, across Eggemoggin Reach to Little Deer Isle and on to the main island. This is altogether a fascinating area. Having had its bridge for 40 years, it could be argued that Deer Isle is no longer an island. But a few hours driving or cruising its byways soon shows this not to be true. It has the same "islandness" one feels on the Fox Islands, or on Swans Island, soon to be discussed. There is a reticent and canny pride here that seems unique to these islanders. When you get to Stonington, the southerly township of the island, all doubt is removed. The village itself is squeezed neatly between a towering cliffy ridge and the harbor, which commands the Deer Isle Thorofare and Merchants Row. It is simply jammed with working watercraft and facilities to meet their needs. A half hour's stroll along the waterfront effectively tells you that the rest of the world is a long way's away and can probably go hang itself!

Sadie the working mare, and *Rusty Nail* the retired lobsterboat **above**, share Greens Island with Heron Neck Lighthouse.

Saddleback Light guards the southern entrance to Eastern Penobscot Bay **below**. Lonely home to seals and the dim memories of storm and trial for the lightkeepers who once lived here (the house has burned down), the place is a vigilant reminder of the sea's indifference to human enterprise.

The ususal visitors' facilities are, of course, available in the area, but special attention should be called to nearby Haystack, one of the finer schools in arts and crafts in the country.

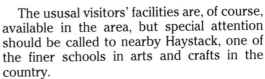

*Isle au Haut*

We get to Isle au Haut by mailboat, passing by Crotch Island, (a huge quarry complex which has recently reopened, famous for its beautiful pink granite; the JFK memorial is made of it), and so on through a surfeit of islands that is almost dazzling in its number and character. For the boatman, this is real knockout country, in the good sense. Though the largest part of Isle au Haut is part of Acadia National Park, centered on Mount Desert Island, 30 miles by sea to the northeast, it does have its

Part of the Fox Islands, Greens
Island was once home to a thriving
community of farmers and
quarrymen. Today it is largely wilderness.

The Acadian uplands of Mount
Desert, here about Jordan Pond, can easily
carry one's imagination to arctic
taiga, the Scottish Highlands, or Southern
Patagonia.

own small residential community. Tourist facilities are nonexistent, though camping arrangements can be made through the Park Service at Mount Desert. Six by three miles, this is a very large parcel of island wilderness, redolent in wildlife and filled with largely uninventoried natural wonders. Cliffs, lakes, deep woods, mountains—all are undeveloped and seldom disturbed. For understandable reasons, Isle au Haut's small township is these days deep in debate over their future policy towards visitors and how to protect this wilderness gem from becoming like the nation's other oversubscribed parts.

## Fox Islands

And so, having surrounded Penobscot Bay, we cast a brief glance out to its center, at the Fox Islands. Thought by local children to look like a great dragon on the chart, this island cluster is rife with natural and social contrasts. The place was first described by Martin Pring in 1603 and afterward enjoyed or suffered most all the same vicissitudes as the other mid-coastal communities—farming and fishing when battle was not being done with Indians or the English. However, by stroke of luck and geology, the southern half of Vinalhaven (named after a land lobbyist in the Massachusetts General Court who helped the early settlers get clear title to their lands) is underlaid with a very pure and evenly textured gray granite. The granite industry began in the late eighteenth century, but it really took off in economic importance after the Civil War, when stream technology created the means, and vigorous urban expansion created the markets, for large-scale exploitation of the resource. On Vinalhaven, then, quarrying (and fishing) distracted the farming effort, and nearly the entire island reverted to forest as up to 2,000 men were at times employed in the pits and sheds. (Today's popuation is around 1,300, total.) Meanwhile, North Haven, without granite, hung on to their agricultural base long enough to be discovered by the rusticators of the late nineteenth century, thus saving their open land. North Haven remains rela-

A hazy summer fog creeps through the Fox Islands Thorofare, and the waterfront of North Haven village **above left** and **below**. An old fishing and boat-building town in its own right, North Haven nevertheless is primarily associated with it very early rusticator cottaging community. It remains a nearly mandatory stopping place for many of the northeast's most prestigious yachtsmen.

Now automated, the lighthouse on Matinicus Rock **above right** is one of the most important marks for large vessels on the coast. This photo shows some of the hardships that its inhabitants once faced—the track was used to hoist stores and groceries!

**Overleaf** Eventide, and part of the windjammer fleet sits to their anchors in Pulpit Harbor, North Haven as the crew and guests sit to sumptuous supper below decks.

**119**

Deep winter at Tarr's Cove, Vinalhaven **above**, in mid-Penobscot Bay, is a place of almost palpable quiet—only chickadees and the occasional kinglet or downy woodpecker interrupt the walker's solitude.

The Maine State Ferry Service's *Governor Curtis* **below** turns on her keel before putting in to the Rockland terminal to discharge and take on cars, trucks and passengers in its regular duty between Vinalhaven and the mainland.

tively open and the pride of swish summer cottages. Vinalhaven is mostly deep woods, but certainly she has her own pride, in lobster fishing. The island's face is to sea, and the 200-odd fishermen of this town are the premiere "crushers" of the coast, commanding fishing bottoms out to sea 40 miles and more. Where other coastal harbors find winter a kind of quiet desolation, Vinalhaven's is still full up with working commercial craft, and the waterfront is a hive of activity. For this reason, the seasonal residents have not converted the town's sensibilities to the rather transient modes of style common elsewhere, much to the satisfaction of permanent and most

seasonal residents alike. Both North Haven and Vinalhaven are served by regular ferries out of Rockland, daily.

The Fox Island Thorofare is the first serious pleasure port of call "downeast," a place to meet or let off passengers and yet feel truly underway, in the midst of a hundred splendid anchorages. To many yachtsmen, this is paradise. And these are the training waters for the famous Hurricane Island Outward Bound School, one of the most creative and successful ventures in alternative education in the country. Here people of all ages and backgrounds, in many different kinds of programs, come away healthier and more self-assured than they ever thought possible. The school, with headquarters in Rockland, takes its place easily and comfortably alongside Bowdoin, the Darling Center, Maine Maritime, and College of the Atlantic, providing first-rate education on the coast of Maine.

Out to sea, Seal and Woodenball Islands, and Criehaven and Matinicus, with their own ancient histories in fishing and settlement, help Matinicus Rock guard Penobscot Bay.

## Quarrying and the Stone Trades

This region is often described as "the rock-bound coast of Maine," and buried within this cliché is reference to one of the area's major historic resources—stone. Geologically, the Maine Coast is composed of thousands of substructures, derived from all three of the major eastern mountain-building processes in prehistoric times, but only the granite and limestone components have had significant economic value. There has been, however, some commercial mining in the coastal zone—copper, zinc, and lead, mostly—and of course sand and gravel deposits are always in demand and thoroughly exploited where they occur.

Millions of years ago, great infusions of granite erupted up through the older volcanic and metamorphic rocks of still earlier times, and when these were later exposed and eventually scrubbed clean by the mighty glaciers of

Tarr's Cove, Vinalhaven . . .
a naturalist's paradise.

A wild iris (blueflag) dresses up the foreground of Woodenball Island, in outer Penobscot Bay **left**. Abandoned summer fishing shacks dot the sedgey hillside in the background.

the Ice Age, all was prepared for much of the landscape we see today along the shore. These granites—white, gray, black, and pinks in hue for the most part—were perfect for quarrying. Their native structure possessed natural cracks, going in two planes, vertical and horizontal, generally at intervals which allowed easy extraction in convenient sizes for the technologies available to the early quarrymen.

Beginning in the late eighteenth century, quarries were established in Penobscot Bay, by Scotsmen primarily, and the stone industry grew from there and thrived for 150 years thereafter. The earliest technology was basic and primitive, by any standard. A large and properly structured granite "dome" was located right next to navigable deep water. Natural cracks in the rock were then cleaned out and filled with dry oak gluts or wedges, and these then *wicked* with water. The expanding wood would slowly open up the cracks and finally the combined forces of all the wedges would break the rocks free. Once free, the generally squared piece of stone would be bailed securely in rope and carefully lowered to the deck of ships waiting below at

the base of the stone face. More than one captain must have looked up at the descending rock and wondered at the competence of whoever had manufactured the rope being used!

Later on, beginning in the 1830s, more remote non-shoreside quarries were opened up, bringing horses and oxen into play. Forge-hardened drills were improved, making extensive drilling practical, as was blasting gunpowder. When steampower was made practical and generally available, the Eastern cities of the nation really took on a new look, for then Maine began to really produce the stone which soon filled not only the urban skyline with buildings and monuments of all kinds but also paved the streets and curbed the walkways. Huge quarries were opened between Port Clyde and Mount Desert, quite literally spewing forth America's cities.

Photographs 100 years old and older show a thousand men at work in one hole—men drilling, rigging, driving, and hauling. Towns like Vinalhaven, in the middle of Penobscot Bay, would have five mutually unintelligible languages spoken—the Yankee fishermen and farmer, Scots-Irish, Finnish and Swedish

**Overleaf** A gray seal on Seal Island. Both harbor seals and gray seals are common along the Maine coast. Seal Island, at the southern entrance to Penobscot Bay, is starkly dramatic and remote.

Low tide at Petit Manan **right**. The light is now automated, but its house structures are used as a scientific observation station by students and faculty from College of the Atlantic in Bar Harbor.

paving cutter, and Italian stone carvers who, day after day, chiseled out the capitals and gargoyles of a thousand buildings. And beginning with that day when they first coughed up blood, they would begin work on their own memorial stones—often of one piece made to look like many. Though some stone is still sold here and there off of so-called "grout banks," and piles of cut stone never delivered, the granite is no longer of economic importance. New processing technologies, using lasers, could change this soon, but in the meanwhile the mighty holes of Tenants Harbor, Spruce head, Hurricane, Vinalhaven and satellites, Crotch Island, and other places remain unutilized, with their ancient equipment rusting away in the surrounding bushes. The holes do provide some of the finest recreational swimming in the Northeast, though.

What was not made of stone in the nineteenth century urban environment was of brick. While brickmaking, *per se*, was not especially important in the coastal economy, the lime necessary for its mortar certainly was. Rockland and Rockport specifically refer in their names to the millions of cubic yards of limestone which were burned in the kilns that once lined their shores. So-called Johnboats, laden with cordword, daily converged on these kilns, as did thousands of cartloads of chunked stone, all to be properly stacked, fired, and crushed into this most necessary building resource. Remnants of the trade can

The bones of an agricultural
past set off a refurbished farmhouse on
Criehaven, otherwise known
as Ragged Island. Once a thriving year-round
fishing town, these days just
a dozen lobstermen and rusticators use their
dwellings in summer only.

A very old granite quarry **center** looks down on its iced-over pond. For swimming in summer, and skating in winter, few places offer so dramatic a backdrop for sport as a Penobscot Bay quarry.

At various times Seal Island **right** has hosted fishing stations, practice bombing by military aircraft and various scientists. A cleft cave undermines the island from these oceanside cliffs to the opposite side.

still be seen along the north shore of Rockland Harbor, and behind the city, between Rockland and Thomaston, of which Rockland was once a part, (called the "Shore Village"), glimpses can be caught of the enormous quarries from which the limestone was extracted.

The regular visitor to these shores soon makes peace with rock and stone. To be sure, there are great sand beaches and strands on the westerly shores, and even some few here and there downeast—precious secrets to those who know of them, but it is the rocks that take on special importance to the experienced Maine buff. Their intricacy, variation, mineral surprises and plain beauty has those who appreciate them soon playing the mountain goat, scrambling along and amongst them, poking into great cracks and staring into a thousand tide pools. While the "hard" shores of Acadia National Park and Mount Desert are perhaps the best known and most frequently visited, a thousand others, as good or better, are in the region, giving special pleasure to those who seek them out by foot or boat.

# The Islands

If today Maine's rivers seem impressive, they nevertheless pale in size and grandeur to what they were 10,000 years ago, when the last great North American ice sheet retreated northward before the onslaught of global climatic warming. What today are our broad marine bays were then mighty river estuaries, raging maelstroms and torrents miles across, filled with megatons of rocks and gravel brought down from the interior highlands. Were you to have stood, then, on one of the Camden Hills, Blue Hill, or Cadillac Mountain and surveyed the summer melt, you would have found yourself in a tundra-taiga environment, such as you find today around the shores of Hudson Bay. You would, perhaps, see a mastodon, giant bison, and maybe, a hunting party of paleo-Indians. But surely you would see the incredible rivers and probably be terrified by them.

The suspended effluvia of the rivers ground down the valleys and broadened them; when the ice had finally melted and the sea level rose, patches of high ground all along the Acadian shoreline were isolated by the invading sea, making Maine's wonderful islands.

The Maine archipelago today contains some 3,000 islands. A bit less than half of these are today simple ledge and barren rock, perches for bird and seal. About 1,700 of them are covered with vegetation, divided more or less equally between so-called "bird-mammal" islands, in sedges, grasses, and shrubs, and "spruce-fir" islands, graced by the boreal forest covers typical of the mainland's upper reaches; the exceptions to this general division occur in Casco Bay, where most of the islands have eastern hardwood covers. In any case, it is a hard heart that does not have a soft place for islands, and those in Maine are extraordinary. But, like so much else that is Maine, her islands have been thought of primarily as resources to be exploited rather than as places dear unto themselves. To be sure, many islands were settled and farmed in early days, but it was a precarious existence.

**Overleaf** A windjammer reaches past Heron Neck Lighthouse, on Greens Island in the Fox Islands. The archipelago's 3,000 islands give the sailing skipper more options than a lifetime of regular cruising can possibly exhaust.

Home and office for the downeast lobsterman and his family **right**. A first glance sees a rustic country scene. A second glance reveals how much effort and capital the fishery requires. Every lobster trap is hand-built, there's a wharf to maintain, and *then* the boat and a hundred trips to sea every year.

Even though the island growing season is a few weeks longer than the mainland, owing to the conservative warming effects of the autumn sea, other aspects of the marine environment have always exposed islanders to severe meteorological threats. In addition, self-defense on islands is nearly impossible, and so the early days often saw the islands swept of white settlement. Even in the late Colonial period, most islanders had to tow the Tory line and suffer the indignities of English requisition. If you've ever wondered where the British Navy got its provisions, while harassing, say, Falmouth and Castine, it was from Maine islands.

Only a dozen genuine island communities remain intact outside of Casco Bay, and of these only Monhegan, Matinicus, Vinalhaven, North Haven, Isleboro, Isle au Haut, Swans, Cranberry, and Frenchboro enjoy regular boat service to and from them. Some two dozen other islands support year-round residents, who get by on their own, but even when it is all added up, it constitutes a mere remnant of what once was a coast-long island culture. Today it is overgrown fields, cellar holes, and silence that reign. Nevertheless, islands remain special places, and islanders special people.

Hearty, hard-working, gregarious and traditionally very skilled, today's islanders find themselves under tremendous pressures to change, to become more like mainlanders. Cottagers are buying up the land, and tourists are invading the village streets, looking for distractions. Some islands have successfully specialized. Monhegan gets its lobster fishing over with by June and then hosts a very large summer artist colony. North Haven and Islesboro set up shop and make a genuine business of its rusticators and cottagers. Vinalhaven and Swans are first and foremost fishing communities, and Beals Island makes a boatbuilder out of a kid whenever it can. Meanwhile, other island towns are caught between historical forces and change; Matinicus, Isle au Haut, and Frenchboro all wonder what the twenty-first century has in store for their future as societies.

Putting people aside, the islands and their importance to wildlife cannot be overstated. First of all, that islands exist at all means that they are surrounded by relatively shoaly bottom, which makes them excellent habitats

**Black Skimmer** This striking black-and-white bird has a bright red beak and is often to be seen skimming along the surface of the water.

The Maine coastal geology is
diverse and complex, a product of at least one
continental collision and three
mountain-building periods. Here the sea
washes over a so-called tumbolo
beach made up of gray, green and jet-black
jasper pebbles, some of gemstone
quality.

Training boats **above** from the Hurricane Island Outward Bound School tie up to Cross Island, for instruction at the Island Institute's Cross Island facility. The school uses more than 150 of the coastal islands in its unique and effective educational programs.

Archaeologists screen-sift through the backdirt of an Indian site in Muscongus Bay **below**. Note the shell fragments in the sifted soil.

for wildlife, especially sea and shore birds' nesting and brooding sites. Great colonies of gull, tern, cormorant, and eider ducks dot the archipelago; puffin, razorbill, petrel and other relatively rare species for the coast enjoy limited, and precarious, island nesting colonies. Many educational and scientific institutions are taking an interest in Maine's islands, with a whale-watch station at Mount Desert Rock, bird-monitoring stations at Little Egg and Petit Manan, and general research programs at Cross, Hurricane, Burnt, and Seal Islands. It is becoming more and more common for, say, a geologist, a botanist, a marine biologist and an archaeologist to quite literally bump into one another on a Maine island!

As mainland citizens discover what islanders, yachtsmen, and scientists have known all along—that islands are beautiful and special places—pressure to protect them mounts. Organizations such as the Maine Coast Heritage Trust, the Maine Audubon Society, and the Nature Conservancy have made concentrated efforts to identify and legally protect critical island habitats from disturbance. Maine's state agencies have taken up their responsibilities on the islands, and several educational institutions, most notably the College of the Atlantic and the Island Institute (part of the Hurricane Outward Bound School) have created a range of research instructional programs specifically for, about, and on the islands.

# NASKEAG POINT TO EASTPORT: THE REAL DOWNEAST

Jericho, Blue Hill, and Union River bays show us the way to Ellsworth. When we have returned back across the Deer Isle Bridge into Sedgewick to rejoin the mainland, a staid quietness seems to fall on the landscape. Our winding roadway passes cluster after cluster of well-formed dwellings—some with smoke curling out the chimney, others either thriving in summer luxuriance or boarded up, depending on the season of our explorations. Perhaps half of the dwellings in this region are now occupied seasonally, giving a pleasant but nevertheless rather melancholy sense to the area. What comes to mind, oddly, is the Chesapeake—its eastern shore also a poignantly melancholy and beautiful area, not yet altogether rejoined with the mainstream of its bayside neighbors. Here and there fishermen and boatbuilders alternate with youngish, somewhat displaced jacks-of-all-trades, a retiree or his widow, an artist or would-be artist, and, not infrequently, just plain old-fashioned Mainer-survivors. It is that sort of area.

But it is also a lovely place at all times of year! Sports-car owners from mid-state come to this peninsula not to speed but simply to let the variegated countryside happen to that union of creature and machine that such roads and country inspire. All the coast is Sunday drive territory, but here a few more stops have been pulled out.

Brooklin and its Naskeag Point find the end of this water-infused place. Just up the road from the point itself, where some of the most important Indian archaeology is going on, are the offices of *WoodenBoat* magazine, a publication dedicated to this oldest of Maine crafts. The magazine has over 100 thousand subscribers nationwide. Writer E.B. White has called this home for most of his life, and these literary proclivities leak out into what is nearly an association of creative spirits in the region, including, inevitably, Blue Hill.

*Blue Hill*

Blue Hill. You'll never guess why it is called that. Hint: most of the time, from any reasonable distance away, it's blue. Route One, the main drag, has given us a glimpse or two, but here on the peninsula it is Blue Hill that first shows us how blueberry barrens are supposed to look. The stark drama of it on a clear day can be breathtaking. In addition, its namesake village is one of the few municipal

Mount Desert Rock **right**, located well out to sea from its namesake, is a study in how stressed and barren an environment can be, and still serve human purpose. Fishermen returning from the Eastern Banks swear by it!

Marvelous contrasts share the nearby countryside, delighting the senses. The Congregational Church of Ellsworth **opposite** presides over a neighborhood only a few miles from dramatically **138** stark blueberry barrens.

Egg Rock, Baker and Great Duck **right** lights help to circumscribe the shimmering waters around Mount Desert Island.

An elderly boat shop tries to hid the 1815 Holt House in Blue Hill **center**. Old house enthusiasts will see that its roof is from a later age, probably added after a now-forgotten nineteenth-century fire.

communities in the nation that has in its entirety been placed on the National Registry of Historic Places. It is stunning! To be sure, the byways around the village are filled with well-heeled patronage, but even at that the locals glow with pride and feel no need to pay homage to anyone but themselves. The community design is excellent.

## Ellsworth

Whether by direct- or shore-route out of Blue Hill, Surry and Ellsworth show us the way to Mount Desert. Ellsworth is one of those inherently splendid Maine towns that has found itself inadvertently to be on the way to somewhere else; and one can say, to some degree, that this is too bad. Not only is the village packed with graceful old homes (most famous, probably, being the Black Mansion) but the cultural amenities here put those of many large communities along the coast to shame. Chamber music, repertory theater, and dance are all gladly celebrated here all year. Its newspaper, the *Ellsworth American*, is generally recognized among professionals to be one of the best small-town newspapers in the nation. Yet the four-and-one-half million (!) annual visitors to Acadia National Park must pass through Ellsworth, whether from the westward or from Bangor, on two-lane roads, leaving the summer Ellsworth a flurry of traffic. Along with Rockland and Belfast, Ellsworth receives nowhere near the respect and appreciation it deserves, as visitors seek merely the quaint and curious that often have so little to do with Maine's true strength—her people.

## Mount Desert

Mount Desert absolutely deserves its fabulous reputation. The whole area is stellar sightseeing and, true to form, the visual delights of it all were, early on, sequestered by wealthy rusticators during the late nineteenth century. What the Cabots did for North Haven, the Rockefellers did here. Until the terrible forest fire of 1947, Bar Harbor was second only to Newport, Rhode Island, for summer social games, and even today both Bar Harbor and

**Overleaf** Sunrise at Mount Desert Island, showing some of the many small islands that dot the entire coast.

141

Egg Rock lighthouse **right**. After many years of waning interest in America's lighthouses, citizen groups nationwide are banding together to prevent total abandonment of their residence facilities, and to preserve or create social roles that lighthouses can usefully carry into the next century.

Northeast Harbor are key places for the development of that rosy glow on many a debutante's autumn facade. These two essentially resort communities are nicely balanced by attractive working towns, Southeast Harbor and Tremont, the former well known for its exquisite yacht-building craftsmanship, the latter a classic fishing town, out of Bass Harbor. The dominant feature is, of course, Acadia National Park, unique in park policy for its charter, which allows citizens not only to bequeath land to the park, but also to land-trade with it. The place continues to grow and improve its holdings all the time without having to parley continuously in Congress. This, naturally, has led to all kinds of squabbles with the local townships, which dislike seeing land alienated from the tax roles. The result, however, is nevertheless extraordinary in that here is a national recreational facility capable of changing with the times.

The great geological gash of Somes Sound makes here the Eastern Seaboard's only true fiord, a long narrow chasm of water reminiscent of British Columbia and the west of Norway. In addition to the usual amenities of well-heeled spas, galleries, and summer stock theater, Bar Harbor is blessed with The College of the Atlantic, a liberal arts college offering the only undergraduate degree to human ecology in the country, and the Jockson Memorial Laboratory, a famous cancer research center notable for its pure-strain laboratory mice.

Three inhabited island clusters are served by ferryboats out of Mount Desert harbors: Swans, out of Bass Harbor–McKinley, the Cranberrys, out of Northeast and Southwest Harbors, and Frenchboro–Long Island, out of Southwest Harbor. All three island groups offer a firm glance at island life that is fast waning as modern transport and communication technology work their ambivalent magic. The image of hard-working fishermen and

Dramatically stark blueberry
barrens dominate the landscape only a few
miles from Ellsworth.

Acadia National Park's shoreline **right**, on Mount Dessert, attracts millions of visitors each year. Here rock and water meet in their eternal challenge.

their families conducting their lives in plain, but charming small cottages and fishhouses, wending their ways by old trails, always in sight of the sea, can yet be found. But modern economic necessity is straining this image, and inexorably the land is being subdivided, and new and different kinds of houses and seasonal camps are going up all the time. Many fishhouses begin to decline as synthetic fishing gear and high-tech equipment become the concern of new fiberglass fishing boats. But the islands, more than elsewhere, have tried to keep the old ways vital. Still, young people, after all, are young people, and the twenty-first century beckons. Even now, Swans Island has re-zoned for tourist development and Frenchboro publicly advertises for young fishermen and their families to move there so that they can maintain a "critical mass" necessary to keep the community viable.

Reluctantly abandoning Mount Desert, we pass back through Trenton, named after the critical Revolutionary War battle in New Jersey, and turn by road through Lamoine, Hancock, Sullivan and Sorrento townships. All four towns have their niceties, to be sure, but it is difficult to characterize towns that are primarily bedroom and seasonal resident towns other than to designate them as such. Clearly, people who have invested time and money into their places love them. The waters are spiced, as are all Maine waterways, and the views in Frenchmans Bay are among the best.

And there is another difficulty that faces the local land traveler—whether to move by road downeast on the coastal Route One, as usual, or to take the short-cut over Route 182 to Cherryfield. Why the confusion? Well, it is because of Tunk Lake.

Baker lighthouse, off Mount Desert **left**, is one of a number of lighthouses that has excited the interest of preservation groups. Unlike many of the lighthouses this one still retains its living quarters. Lighthouse buffs call themselves "believers."

**Overleaf** A copper-colored dusk at Schoodic Peninsula silhouettes part of the local fleet.

147

## The Tunk Lake District

From the coastal route at Hancock there is an opportunity to cut across the main through a most unusual place, the Tunk Lake District. Here is a veritable textbook "birch-beech-maple" forest that is unusual for its stand purity and maturity. Until you see it, you are bound to wonder why a stretch of woods in a state that is 90 percent forest would be especially cited as a byway for the coastal traveler. But a glance tells you how special it is, for here is the most northerly occurrence of this forest type in the country, and a perfect, exemplary one at that. While not virgin growth in the usual sense of the term, it is fully mature, and the long, thick and straight stems of the trees will instantly show the intelligent youngster how a classic hardwood forest is supposed to look. Except in certain parts of the Cumberland and Piedmont, such woods are now rare in the United States. Tunk Lake is set in its midst, a crystal-clear and deep body of water and a fine gem for this precious arboreal setting.

## The Coastal Forest

Trees. Trees everywhere, all over the place. To fly down the coast on a clear day is to gaze on trees, only a little interrupted by roadways, farms, and villages. If it is not trees, it is a tangle of shrubs and bushes. But everywhere vegetation abounds on the coast of Maine. Along the mainland coastal routes, the basic tree covers are extensions of the "eastern hardwood-pine covers," typical to those found to the west and south of the coast—mixed species according to their soils, history, and sun-exposures, the number of species in the natural mix slowly diminishes as the traveler moves downeast. In the higher uplands, places of poor sun exposure, and on many of

the islands, the hardwood forests give way entirely to spruce-fir boreal covers—evergreen woods of white, red, and black spruce, with an understory of balsam fir, which here and there can be found in pure stands. These fir stands tend to be young, covering the edges of reverting fields, and the locals heavily prefer them at Christmastime. The smell of balsam *means* Christmas to many a coastal youngster!

Wherever moisture tends to collect, alders

**Above** Conifers and deciduous hardwoods fringe one of the many bays which bring a placid beauty to Maine's jagged coastline.

The Blue Nose ferry **below**, out of Bar Harbor, takes passengers, vehicles and cargo daily across the eastern Gulf of Maine and outer Bay of Fundy to Nova Scotia. It saves a long day's driving, and offers some genuine sea-time to passengers, including the right to gamble in international waters.

Maine shorelines are endlessly
varied, and for this reason offer very different
advantages and problems to
fishermen. Here, at one place on the
Jonesports shore, a fisherman
must build his wharf far out over the shoals
yet, at another place, nearby
boats can nudge right up to the land.

tend at first to predominate, followed by larches (locally called hackmatack, or plain "hack"), and wherever the land has been either recleared or burned, white and gray birch and the red (soft) maples commonly sprout up to cover the landscape. Along the edges of drier places, the aspens and closely related poplar species shiver and shake in the breeze and add a splendid yellow to the autumn landscape.

The original coastal forests were a good deal richer in variety than those we see today. In addition to those we typically find today, wild walnut, butternut and the hickories were much more common. Many elms, the white-woods, such as tulip, and American chestnut occurred regularly; today, they are represented only in very special places. Certain forest types, rather common in southern New England and beyond, these days enjoy only remnant islands of forest stand—perhaps the most notable being the marvelous mature beech-birch-maple forest surrounding Tunk Lake, west of Cherryfield.

The usual coastal vistas of a hundred years ago included very few trees, and thinking about the living requirements and economy of those times makes this easily understood. For starters, 80 percent of all Americans then lived on farms (today it is less than five percent), New England and the coast of Maine included. Most transport, and all farm work, was accomplished by horse and oxen. They required vast quantities of grass and hay grown on pastures and fields, the hay itself in competition with grains and produce crops. What woods remained, for *wood* uses, were heavily exploited. Not only was every household, whether rural or in town, at least partly dependent on trees for their heat and cooking fuel but domestic wood was also continually in demand for construction, tools, furniture and implements, and for cash. Faraway cities needed huge quantities of wood, and local coastal industries, such as charcoal-making, limeburning, and shipbuilding consumed wood of many types in awesome fashion.

So most of the forest covers along the coast of Maine today are "reverted" forests, which cover ground cleared of tree growth at least once, and some as many as three times, since the period of first settlement. As one travels

A gray "soft" day in late autumn **left** reveals shoreside birches, aspens, and young spruces, all of which tell the canny observer that this was once agricultural land, probably pasture for livestock.

The **quaking aspen** takes its name from the near-ceaseless fluttering of its broad leaves.

**Overleaf** Scientists in many fields find a bounty of things to study along the Maine Coast. Under clouds proclaiming wind the next day, a Smithsonian Institute research vessel probes and delves into the secrets of Dyers Bay.

**Above** A commercial lobster-buying wharf at Beals Island basks in the late afternoon sunlight. The boats are in, the skiffs are pulled up onto the float — the working day is over.

Lobsterboats, shown **below** in the harbor at Corea, can cost their owners as much as thirty-five thousand dollars — before paying out for the expensive equipment needed to catch the lobster.

the byways of the coast from west to east, a common pattern of view is immediately discernible; alternating patchy farmland generally interrupted by large areas of mixed hardwoods and pine, and, occasionally, by developed strips leading into and out of elder village centers. As you continue to journey beyond Penobscot Bay, more and more boreal species—spruces, fir, and larch—enter the forest mix, until east of Mount Desert, they come to predominate.

Most of these woods date from about 1910, when the last heyday of coastal farming ended, giving way to the vast midwestern granary and a developing national transportation network. Except for some truck farming here and there, and of course dairy pasturage and hay crops, coastal farming has progressively languished for the past 70 years. This leaves the bulk of coastal country acreage in woodlot covers, which, since the early 1970s, have increased in their desirability and utility as nearly every year-round household rediscovered the practicality of wood heat.

Now and again the coastal woods have suffered from spectacular forest fires, most notably the Great Bar Harbor fire of 1947 on Mount Desert Island. These days it shows its ravages in great panoramas of stunted reverted growths and grand cellar holes, where once elegant country estates cottages loomed over large and well-tended grounds.

While the truly significant timber interests of the state are justifiably associated with the interior uplands, the coastal woods have from time to time been heavily exploited. It is the nature of spruce wood to have long and very strong fibers, perfect for the manufacture of paper. It is also the nature of spruce to suffer the occasional ravages of the spruce budworm, which has in the past decimated whole generations of these trees, especially those of the interior plantations. (Plantations, in the New England sense, mean unincorporated and wild, not the southern sense of cultivated.) Coastal forests are not so prone to this pest, and so periodically after such a blight, some of the large timber outfits come to the coast for their wood, as they did in the 1950s in response to the blight attacks of the late teens and early twenties and as they will again in the 1990s, in response to the outbreaks in the 1930s. Looking far backward and well forward in time is a necessary habit of the wood-products industries.

Recalling that date mentioned before—1910—when most of the shoreside forests began introduces a problem: the boreal species are not long-lived, and 70 years of age represents the apex of their longevity and condition. After that they become more prone to disease, develop heart-rot, or simply fall down. The coastal soils are not especially deep, and much of them were over-grazed and over-cultivated during the nineteenth century.

Corea's small harbor provides
a textbook picture of how the Maine
lobsterboat can vary in size
and form, yet give no confusion as to what
they are.

They are not capable of supporting very large trees that have to endure high oceanic winds in winter and certainly not those of hurricane force, which a couple of times a century have had a way of coming ashore over these waters. The Maine archipelago is especially endangered. Some thousand tree-covered islands support over two billion board feet of timber, most fully mature, untested by hurricane in nearly 30 years, on very thin island soils! Waiting for the paper industry's "fiber crunch," expected in the 1990s, is these days a nip-and-tuck affair for island and coastal forest owners. Which will come first, they wonder, a good market with a cooperative industrial technology or a devasted landscape of useless wood that cannot be sold and may be susceptible to terrible fires at the next summer's drought to come along?

## The Coastal Woods

Meanwhile, the Maine woods is the pride and joy of all who live here and many who visit. From Kittery to Eastport, it is its continually changing character that makes it a kind of tendable wilderness, perfect for a variety of game and wildlife, woodlot management, natural history preservation, recreation, education and research. Like its fisheries, the coastal woods is the "finest kind" of wealth a people and region can possess.

texture of Gouldsboro), popular among summer cottagers and yachtsmen alike. Prospect, Birch, and Schoodic harbors are all good "lee" harbors in summer, offering protection from the prevailing southwest breezes, as is Winter Harbor on the western side of the Schoodic Peninsula, famous for never having iced-over, even in the severest seasons. The road that circumscribes Schoodic Peninsula offers some of the finest panoramic driving on the entire coast.

## The Schoodic Peninsula

Back on Route One, or crossing the mouth of Frenchmans Bay by boat, we come to Winter Harbor and Gouldsboro, together making up a lovely peninsula (indeed, Maine author Louise Dickinson Rich's book, *The Peninsula*, is a charming story of the history and social

## Washington County

And so into Washington County. As a region, it is one of the earliest-explored in North America, yet one of the most sparsely settled. It is one of the poorest counties in the land, yet, oddly, it has one of the highest savings-to-

Moose Peak Light **left**, located in Mistake Island off Jonesport, is one of America's many navigational beacons that have lost their attendant houses.

**American Sycamore** This magnificent tree, found in moist areas throughout the east, is the tallest broad-leaf tree species in the United States.

**Overleaf** The Barrens, of Washington County, are stark landscapes that speak eloquently of the sub-artic environment.

Nash Light's square tower **right**, off cape Split, guides Washington County navigators to safety through complex water.

income quotients, according to financial institution records. Its wilderness areas seem boundless, and the map confirms what the auto windshield reveals—vast expanses of land untouched by human activity, save here and there one will find lumbering and wild-blueberry harvesting.

The communities of Steuben, Milbridge, Harrington and Addison seem, on the outside, simply to continue the pattern of seasonal homes punctuated by small fishing harbors and the splendid views that grace any journey on the coast of Maine. But there are differences, most of them having to do with the more stressed economic and meteorlogical environment in these downeast waters. Much of this area has a scrubby, almost subartic feel.

Winter comes sooner and stays longer, and cultural features—stores, shops, and restaurants—are obviously fewer and further between. The aquatic views from the many points of land have an austere quality that can, on clear days, ravish the eye and mind. Edges are delineated in a way that sometimes seem hallucinatory in its shimmering lucidity.

The village of Steuben is named after Baron Friedrich von Steuben, a Prussian officer who helped General Washington instill some modicum of discipline into the often rowdy troops of the Continental Army. Milbridge is home of Jasper Wyman & Sons, the world's largest processor of blueberries—Washington County's crop is the world's largest, usually between 15 and 20 million

At Bucks harbor, gulls sit atop
weir-spiles in patient expectation of events to
come. Bird and man alike must
outwait the fog, as witnessed by boats at their
mooring.

For generations, keepers and their families tended towers like this one at Moose Peak **right**. Now their memory fades in the mists of bureaucratic indifference and automation.

pounds annually. The Narraguagus River, which empties into Pleasant Bay at Milbridge, is one of the great return rivers for the Atlantic salmon. And Harrington and Addison, which come next, quietly overlook their waters through the seasonal round in remote diffidence.

For more than a decade Jonesport has placed itself very thoroughly on the map by being home to one of the two great annual lobsterboat races on the coast of Maine. Nearby Beals Island has been one of the primary development centers of very fast lobsterboats for many years, and so it is fitting that each summer the bridge span between the mainland at Jonesport and Beals Island becomes clotted with spectators from all up and down the coast to view these extraordinary working craft, some of which, stripped of fishing gear, move through the water at over 40 miles per hour. Jonesport also has the good fortune to overlook Chandler Bay and its glorious Rocque Island, the final downeast anchorage goal for many cruising yachts, including yacht club flotillas.

Rocque Bluffs and Point of Main, in Machiasport, overlook the island, and from these places the general belief that "Rocque" is a corruption of the word *rogue* is satisfactorily confirmed, for this whole area was well known as a pirate haven in early times. The prominences are ideal for surveying the seaway entrances to Machias Bay, which in turn has many little coves and bights offering perfect protection and cover for whatever "scurvy lots" might choose to use them. While not so historically famous as Castine, the Machiases (Machiasport, Machias, and East Machias) have stories to tell that are nearly as bloody and long. Early earthwork fortifications of old Fort Machias now support picnics at the Fort O'Brien Memorial (a later fort at the ancient location), and it was here that, quite literally, the American Navy was born, in response to the 1775 successful attack by the Machias citizenry against the English armed schooner *Margaretta*. Word of the skirmish in the Continental Congress spurred them to create an official seagoing force.

Other Machiasian features include the Burnham tavern, built in 1770 and recognized as the oldest colonial structure east of the Penobscot, and Picture Rock, where Indian petroglyphs (rock carvings), which are rare in

Maine, can be seen. The outback of this whole region is blueberry bog country of the highest order.

## Salt Marshes and Barrens

People who must, or choose to, look out often to sea develop a taste for a landscape others may think to be barren or desolate. When there are few things to look at, what there *is* to look at becomes very important, whether it is another boat on the horizon, birds feeding, or a hawk circling over field mice. The upshot of this is that Maine coastal people do not really believe in desolation. They know that under the uniform surface, the sea is teeming with marine life; the barren hillside is rife with life and production; and the salt marsh is a nursery for millions of marine fry, birds, and food supply for thousands of creatures.

The Maine coast has had fewer problems protecting its salt marshes and barrens than have other places, in large part because the common wisdom of the coast derives closely from the historic uses of them and from plain intelligent observation. The term "salt-water farm" is no stranger here. Salt-marsh hay contains nine times per acre the nutrients required in proper grazing than does good, dry-land, terrestrial grass, and Maine people who have experienced and benefited from this fact are not yet dead! Furthermore, kids who are allowed to putter around in boats alone in the harbor have always first been allowed to putter around in boats on marshes. Kids learn to see and enjoy the countless small fish to be observed there and eventually to connect the fisheries of his adulthood with the little fish seen in his youth. Finally, there is the gunning season, and *good* hunters know what is good for ducks, with or without the bird-ecology-nature enthusiasts on their backs for other reasons.

The marshes of the shore provide the kindergarten for many of the gulf of Maine's adult creatures. The odd thing about them is that they are seldom viewable from the

**Left** Blueberry barrens abut the northern spruce forests. Once a year a lonely shed becomes a counting house and paymaster's shack, where the huge blueberry harvests are tallied and made ready for processing.

Blueberry plants, often as here
mixed with wild strawberry, are very hardy,
and will grow anywhere a tiny
bit of acid soil offers itself, preferably on
boggy ground. Every third year
or so, depending on weather, Maine
blueberries produce very large
bumper crops.

A red ochre farmhouse, horse
team, and pasture on lovely Roque Island.
Many contemporary islanders
have found much good sense and satisfaction
in traditional means of conducting
life. The house is beautifully sited to receive
the full benefit of the sun, yet
protection from the ocean winds.

West Quoddy Head Lighthouse **right** receives a much-needed overhaul for further duty. Modern electronic navigation notwithstanding, a man, his eyes, and a light to see by will never be replaced.

coastal roadways. Here and there along the major arteries—the Turnpike, Route 95, and Route One, you can catch a glimpse of a few, but almost all watersheds along the coast possess their backwater salt marsh as part of their estuaries. These constitute a precious resource and benefit to the regions that have them, and by fecund extension, to this whole region of the Atlantic.

From just East of Bucksport, Maine's famous blueberry barrens begin to appear, on the occasional hillside at first, whole countrysides at a time, downeast in Washington County. While popularly known as "blueberry barrens" on account of the toothsome commercial crop they provide, in fact they are generally the surface covers for vast *peat bogs*. Thousands of years ago, when the region was in a transition period between a post-glacial tundra-taiga cover and the boreal forests of today, there was a mixed hardwood cover, probably much like Southern Siberia today, that regularly burned. This repeated burning eventually consumed a large portion of humic (derived from humus) organic matter in the soil, releasing enough iron molecules to create a leached "iron pan," through

which water could not percolate downward. Following this, as surface plants died, they would fold down into the humic soil where the waterbogged condition of the soil would arrest the rotting process. This is what causes peat formation—the accumulation of incompletely rotted plants—mostly mosses, fern, sedges, and heathers. Peat that is found near the surface is what gardeners know as peat moss. However, as peat accumulates in dead deposits, the lower layers of the material become ever-more chemically reduced to its carbon components, until it becomes a very soft, coal-like substance. Coal, in fact, is simply metamorphosed peat from buried peat beds of very ancient times. Many Irish country people regularly mine their peat deposits for heating and cooking fuel, and Maine's great bogs are currently being studied for their electrical generation potential in the region.

As they are, the bogs are a magnificent sight, and a walk up into them will reward the traveler with some of the essence of primal landscape, of a rich desolation in which native Mainers find much beauty and introspective solace against a complicated and often pestiferous modern world.

Avery Rock Light (a new-style light) **left** stands sentinel off Cape Split.

*Cutler*

*Cobscook Bay*

Beyond the Machiases and before the towns encircling Cobscook Bay and the end of our sojourn, comes ominous Cutler. Almost entirely wilderness, known only for its excellent protective harbor (popular among deep-sea fishing vessels as a hideout from gales), Cutler is the location of the world's most powerful broadcasting facility. Its more than two dozen, thousand-foot towers and great domes loom over the skyline—military, secret, commonly understood to be the central nervous system for the nation's undersea submarine tele-network. The stark natural beauty here contrasts utterly with the electromagnetic muscle of our most sophisticated abilities. There is symmetry in the fact that we began our coastal portrait in Kittery, where subs are made, and end it so close to where Kittery's product is instructed moment-by-moment.

While not nearly so large as most of Maine's other bays, Cobscook Bay is surely the most complex. With Lubec on one side of the mouth and Eastport on the other, the two are separated by only three miles, but the roadway connecting them is over 40 miles long! And the shoreline around the bay must be at least 250 miles around from town to town, so indented and crinolated is the tideline. Both towns are essentially fishing and canning (herring) towns; these days, both are relatively depressed. They vie with one another over which is the most easterly town in the United States—Lubec officially gets the distinction because of its mile-long West Quoddy Head, the village itself beating out Eastport by a matter of perhaps a few yards. Nevertheless, the United States Weather Bureau's daily phrase, "Kittery (or Rockland) to Eastport..." contradicts Lubec, and so Eastport advertises

Libby Light **right**, traditional in style, offers an architectural contrast to its Washington County neighbor, the modern Avery Rock lighthouse.

itself as the town "where morning begins."

From Lubec a bridge goes over to Campobello Island and so into Canada, and it is well known as the place FDR called home in summer before he became president. But for our purposes, driving over the bridge or cruising by boat over to and around it, it is fascinating to see the cultural differences that two modern societies have created on the basis of something so mundane as national fisheries policy. Campobello villages, harbors, and boats are neat, trim, and observably prosperous. A few miles away, in the United States towns, there is much evidence of towns being down on their luck, verging, at times, on squalor. Canada subsidizes fisheries. We do not. But, for all that, both Lubec and Eastport (and the towns of Edmonds, with its fine Moosehorn National Wildlife Refuge), Dennysville, Pembroke, and Perry, which lie along the road between them, make up real rubbernecking country for the auto traveler. There is a hardiness in the community *visage* that is undeniable, and any reflection at all gives the urban and suburbanite conscience a twinge of wonder and admiration combined. With Passamaquoddy Bay just outside of Cobscook Bay, and tides ranging up to 30 feet, there is an inherently radical quality to things. It is a sense that here in this beautiful, stark and plaintive land nature is not controlled out of neglect, but rather because here it cannot be controlled, absurd Canadian notions to create a huge tidal-generation facility further to the east notwithstanding.

There are 20-odd miles of coastal road up the shore of Passamaquoddy Bay to Calais, where mainland access to Canada is offered, but the psychological end of the Maine coast is at Eastport. Calais is oddly cosmopolitan, probably as a result of the many different kinds of people waiting to get over the border who must negotiate to do so for various reasons. There is not the "Maine coastal" aspect to it in the sense we have discussed. Technically, Calais is the end, but at Eastport, back down the road, our portrait, as such, ends.

Two-Bush lighthouse is one
of two that directs boatmen into and through
the Mussel Ridge Channel, between
Seal and Rockland Harbors, at Owls Head.

## Picture Credits

Peter Ralston: pp.6, 9, 13, 14, 18/19 (left), 22/23, 28/29, 30, 31, 32/33 (top, bottom), 45, 47 (top, bottom left), 52, 53, 56 (top, centre, bottom), 57, 58/59, 60/61 (top, top right, centre right, bottom), 62/63, 65, 66 (top, centre), 67, 68/69, 70, 71, 72/73, 76/77 (left, centre, bottom), 78/79, 84, 86/87, 88/89, 90/91 (top), 92, 93, 94/95 (centre, right), 97 (top, centre, bottom right), 98, 100, 101 (top), 102/103, 104/105, 114/115 (top, bottom), 116, 118/119 (right), 124, 125, 126/127, 128, 129, 130/131 (left), 132/133, 136 (top, bottom), 138, 140/141 (left), 142/143, 144, 147, 150/151 (bottom), 159, 162, 163, 164/165, 169, 170, 171, 172, 173

Ian Howes: pp.10/11, 42/43 (centre), 64, 82/83 (bottom), 96, 99, 101 (bottom), 106, 108/109 (centre, bottom right), 110, 111, 139, 140/141 (right), 145, 146, 152, 160/161, 166/167, 168

Gordon Lutz: pp.17, 18/19 (right), 20/21, 28/29 (top right, bottom left, bottom centre), 47 (centre), 82/83 (bottom), 112/113, 118/119 (top, bottom), 120/121, 122/123 (bottom), 130/131 (centre), 136, 154/155

Marilyn Lutz: pp.122/123 (top), 150/151 (top)